The Liquid Continent

A Mediterranean Trilogy

Volume II

Venice

by
Nicholas Woodsworth

HAUS PUBLISHING
London

Copyright © 2008 Nicholas Woodsworth

First published in Great Britain in 2008 by Haus Publishing
Limited, 26 Cadogan Court, Draycott Avenue, London SW3 3BX
www.hauspublishing.co.uk

The moral rights of the author have been asserted.

A CIP catalogue record for this book is available from the British
Library

ISBN 978-1-905791-45-3

Typeset in Garamond 3 by MacGuru Ltd
Printed and bound by Graphicom in Vicenza, Italy
Jacket illustration courtesy of Ania McKay (© 2008 Ania McKay)
Interior drawings courtesy of Jaroslaw Dobrowolski
(© 2008 Jaroslaw Dobrowolski)

To Michael Holman, ever steady

One

I shifted my backside on the cold, hard bench of a Cairo bus station. There were times when I wished I'd done my travelling a century or more before. 1872 would have suited me fine. In that year Monsieur J Frugoli, Principal Agent of the Messageries Maritimes steamline company at Alexandria, posted the following tariffs for its Syrian Service, departing fortnightly on Saturdays:

From Alexandria to: (in French Francs)	1st Class	2nd Class	3rd Class
Port Said	45	32	19
Jaffa	78	59	30
Beirut	110	82	40
Tripoli	135	101	50

Latakia	155	117	60
Alexandretta	182	138	69
Mersin	207	157	77
Rhodes	306	231	118
Smyrna	377	284	148
Mitilini	407	308	155
Dardanelles	428	323	166
Gallipoli	436	329	168
Constantinople	469	354	182

It was a dream voyage. It wasn't so much the idea of first-class comforts that made me envious, although I was sure that even a third-class ticket with Messageries Maritimes would have brought more comfort than the bus I was about to board. What seemed almost miraculous were the destinations on offer. I would have gladly travelled deck-class on bread and water to sail into these Levantine ports one after the other. Never mind the leaps in transport technology that lay far in the future – in Monsieur Frugoli's time it was much easier getting around the eastern Mediterranean than it is today.

If a Saturday departure didn't suit, the French maritime company wasn't the only one to stop at the harbours dotting the great curved arc of the sea. The Khedival Mail Line, Lloyd's Austrian and the Russian Steam Navigation and Commercial Company were among others offering similar services along these coasts. But where were they all now? I had checked and re-checked. There was a summer ferry-service to Brindisi and Venice, but that was months away. Short of smuggling myself aboard a freighter, it was impossible to get out of Alexandria by sea. In the end I had bought a ticket from the East Delta Bus Lines – hardly a name with the same kind of romantic resonance – and was headed to a seaport not even on the Mediterranean.

Such were the kinds of choices left to travellers in a politically-fraught Middle East – for anyone who had drawn the line at flying there weren't many options available. Then again, there probably weren't all that many people these days who actually wanted to see a succession of old port-cities in the eastern Mediterranean. But I did.

I'd spent most of the winter in Alexandria, and it had only given me more of an appetite to carry on around the coast to other ports of the eastern Mediterranean. Some of these ports, like distant Istanbul and even more distant Venice, were every bit as mythic as Alexandria – these were cities whose grand historical reputations had sustained them through the ages, even if physically or functionally they had changed beyond recognition. Other, lesser ports, places with lesser histories behind them, might have become forgotten backwaters or even crumbled altogether. But, still, I wanted to see them too.

It had something to do with the allure of the Mediterranean Sea, a pull I found almost impossible to resist. It wasn't just any Mediterranean I was attracted to. Settled in France not far from the sea, I had little feeling at all for that over-crowded, over-glamorised section of the French coast, the Côte d'Azur. Who can feel drawn to time-shares and package holidays and resort towns with nightmare summer parking? In my part of the world I found the working ports, places like Marseilles and Toulon, far more attractive. And the eastern end of the sea, as far as I was concerned, was more attractive still.

What was it that made old and shabby water-front places so appealing? Partly it was pure physical enjoyment. I liked being around ships and busy harbours and exotic crowds. I liked the vibrant physical sensations of Mediterranean seaports – the sun, the bright colours, strong flavours, heady smells, the energy of sea and wind. And just as much as these things themselves, I enjoyed being around people who also enjoyed them. I found that Mediterraneans – Eastern or Western, Arab or European – had a kind of connection, a direct and immediate engagement with the surrounding world. It gave them a special kind of vitality that sometimes made more northern peoples – people like me – look half-hearted and calculating in their enthusiasms. I liked the simple delight Mediterraneans took in life.

But there was something apart from the pure pleasure, something that the weathered sea-walls and rusty docks of these old places barely hinted at. Where did this lively connection with the world come from in the first place? You had to scratch down below the surface to find clues and suggestions. If Mediterraneans were still engaged with the world perhaps it was because their port-cities had been engaged with the world for thousands of years. The old harbours on this sea had been the vibrant global cities of their age.

It was maritime trade had made them the sophisticated places they once were. Dynamic and enterprising, more commercial and open in attitude than their hinterland capitals, they'd *had* to be outward-looking – it was trade from over the seas, that constant exchange with foreign ports across the water, on which their livelihood depended. But that same openness to the outside world had given the great port-cities more than just mercantile sophistication. It gave them cultural sophistication, too. For the ships that unloaded material goods inevitably delivered whole cargoes of invisible goods as well – everything from spiritual philosophy to trends in the pop-music of the day. It was the synthesis of foreign ideas, the simultaneous dockside blending of the habits of countless different seaside places, that made

the old Mediterranean world what it was – a cosmopolitan, globalised world.

And that, as much as the Mediterranean's passing
physical pleasures, was what interested me. Despite
today's high-tech definition, the World Wide Web is
nothing new. It has existed in different forms and in
different ages for a very long time, and the eastern Mediterranean was its birthplace. In Alexandria I'd strolled
among the hidden remains of the planet's earliest globalised city, the first metropolis to be founded on a
universal theme. And that alone had shown me that our
own ideas of globalisation – we believe we've invented
the concept – are not the only ones possible.

But apart from Alexandria there were other old
Mediterranean ports which had gone their own route,
cities with other objectives which long ago had
developed their own versions of globalisation. Venice,
the greatest trading state the Mediterranean has
ever known, had developed a distinctly commercial
approach to the question. As Constantinople, Istanbul
had sat at the centre of a vast empire and used ideas of
globalisation to its own multicultural ends. Each port

in between, too, had had its own needs and methods, and I was hungry to see them all.

Now, with appetite whetted and long, warm spring days stretching ahead, the entire coastline beckoned. But already I knew that the dozen places listed by Monsieur Frugoli posed a dozen different logistical problems. Long ago I'd acknowledged I wasn't going to see Jaffa, Haifa or any other port in Israel. Twitchy travel relations between Arabs and Israelis – matters of visas, passport stamps and closed borders – simply made it too complicated. In fact, just getting to the Mediterranean coast north of Israel was difficult enough.

You could cross the Sinai Peninsula by road, but once on the other side you couldn't get over the top of the Gulf of Aqaba to Jordan – the port of Elat and a five-mile coastal stretch of Israeli territory barred the way. Instead, you had to drive south down the coast of the Gulf, and halfway to the Red Sea catch a boat north again at Nuweiba; once back up the Gulf, it deposited its passengers on the far side of Israeli territory in the Jordanian city of Aqaba.

I wasn't actually looking forward to an all-night bus ride, or even to this leg of the trip as a whole. It seemed an awfully roundabout way to go, and the journey was known to be tough and full of delays – getting from Cairo to Aqaba, less than 250 miles as the crow flies, often took twenty-four hours or more. That came to an average of just ten miles an hour.

It was a speed considerably slower, I calculated, than that of the standard military camel charge. In the Arab uprising of the First World War Lawrence of Arabia had once thundered into Aqaba at the head of hundreds of mounted and determined tribesmen. They were in a hurry, hurtling towards the post-Ottoman independence that Lawrence had promised them. In the end his efforts failed. But something at least could be said for that thundering charge – a direct and lightening-fast advance on the city had to have been a good deal more satisfying than this back-and-forth trundling about. I boarded the East Delta bus wishing that Lawrence – or even better, Monsieur Frugoli – were still in charge of things.

We left Cairo at eleven o'clock in the evening, a

spaghetti of suburban motorways finally leading to a straight, two-lane highway that was almost deserted. Outside there was nothing but a quarter-moon and dimly lit roadside scrub. Occasionally we pulled over, waiting for no discernible reason before rumbling back onto the highway. Once we dropped down into a long, brightly lit concrete tunnel, a passage which I assumed ran beneath the Suez Canal. The only remarkable thing was the desert cold. The bus was unheated, and by two o'clock it wasn't far from freezing outside. Inside, passengers huddled into the folds of their long *galabiyas,* wrapped lengths of cloth around their heads, and fell asleep. Mouths gaped, limbs protruded into aisles in prolonged poses of rigor mortis. In the sickly yellow glimmer of the bus's ceiling lights we looked like zombies from *Night of the Living Dead.*

We stopped at Taba, the border crossing just a couple of miles from the Israeli town of Elat. A few passengers got down, an Egyptian policeman checked passports, and we turned south to drive alongside the Gulf of Aqaba.

In the distance across the head of the gulf we could

see two twinkling masses – the city lights of Elat and Aqaba. At the same time daylight was beginning to swell in the east. It revealed the road we were travelling, a winding strip of tarmac squeezed between water and bone-dry hills of bare rock. On the far side of the gulf, too, the desert ranges of Saudi Arabia climbed sharply away from the shore. But not even this deep, narrow fold in the earth could hide away from day forever. Just outside Nuweiba the sun's rim appeared over the mountains and the whole world – sea, sky and rock – was suffused with light. For a few moments even the craggiest headland glowed a soft and delicate bonbon pink.

Nuweiba straggled alongside the sea, a town of low, white concrete buildings and sand-blown streets just a couple of blocks deep. The bus came to a halt by the harbourside. The zombie passengers abruptly awoke, hustled themselves off the bus and disappeared. Where to, I have no idea; perhaps they knew a good place to remain comatose for the six hours that remained before the sailing to Aqaba. That left just the foreigners. With our bags slung from our shoulders we wandered into a waterfront café – in reality no more than bits of ragged canvas hung over a wooden frame – and ordered tea.

There were four of us. We were all from different places, but in the way of travellers come together by chance in strange places we immediately formed a group.

Lotfi, confident and outgoing, immediately became our leader. He spoke little English but excellent French. He had a pleasing, cheerful manner and didn't hesitate to use it – he could charm anyone to pieces in five minutes. Conscious or not, it was a trick that came in useful. Lotfi was Tunisian, a buyer and a seller. When pressed as to exactly what it was that he bought and sold he was evasive. But his business took him all around the shores of the Muslim Mediterranean. This was his fourth trip to Damascus.

Lotfi travelled light. Apart from a small holdall he didn't have much more than the leather jacket and the clothes he stood up in. The rest of us were bleary-eyed and tired. Lotfi, who was thirty-five but looked ten years younger, was clear-eyed and fresh. He was now five days out of Tunis and moving fast. In order to cut down on expenses and avoid hotel costs he travelled day and night, and hoped to be in Damascus in the next thirty-six hours. Apart from ten-minute catnaps, he claimed he'd hardly slept on this trip at all, and I believed him. He was a natural-born traveller and trader, deft and self-assured in his life on the road, and it pleased him in a way that no sedentary occupation could. I doubt that what Lotfi did was entirely legal, but it didn't stop me liking him.

I liked him even more when I saw the way he looked out for Jimmy. Jimmy was a tall, gangly twenty-year-old Iraqi with a wispy bit of beard on his chin and a prominent Adam's apple. When he spoke he surprised you because he had a reedy, falsetto voice that was pitched higher than most girls'. He was a Christian Arab – Maronite or Syrian Orthodox, I cannot remember which, but at any rate had been brought up in one of those isolated churches that has persisted and survived in the Middle East for centuries. He was goofy about God, and had a touching belief that anyone nominally Christian was automatically a good and trustworthy person. It made you fear for him.

The fact that he felt he had some sort of divine backup only put him at risk, for he was setting off down a murderous road. Through an evangelist Christian connection Jimmy's father was working in a supermarket in Tennessee. But Jimmy, who until now had avoided the Iraq war by staying with his uncle in Cairo, was on his way home to his mother in Baghdad. Lotfi promised Jimmy he would get him as far as Amman, but when he turned east he would be on his own. He had a stack of documents, every necessary paper neatly wrapped in a plastic bag with elastic bands, but he was very nervous.

I sometimes wake up at night and wonder if Jimmy made out all right. As soon as he discovered I was from what he called a 'Christian nation' he dived into the inside breast pocket of his jacket to present me with a card – there was a calendar on one side and a blurry three-colour print of Jesus, hands outstretched in welcome, on the other. But it was Jimmy's physical gesture that concerned me. It was too abrupt, and I hoped he never tried that particular icebreaker with a nervous American soldier at a roadblock. If he did, the world would be one Christian short.

The fourth member of our little band also presented me with a card as we sat sipping tea in Nuweiba's rosy morning light. I looked at the picture on it, compared it to the man in front of me, and looked at the picture again. It showed a pale face with lustrous black curly hair, an enormous moustache and a sort of Sergeant-Pepper uniform – a silver ceremonial sword and big red pasteboard epaulettes with lots of braid, medals and ribbons. It made me want to laugh out loud, but I didn't, for there was no doubt about it – it was a picture of the man in front of me.

'Alsheik Adam Mohammed Amin', I read the name under the photo, and he smiled and nodded. 'Da!' he said enthusiastically, pointing at his chest. And that is as far as we got, for Amin spoke Chechen and Russian, and shared no other language with any of us.

He was a neat little man barely five and a half feet

tall, and for this journey he was in civilian dress – a beautiful sheepskin coat with the wool turned inside and a curious brimless cap of the same stuff. But there was no doubting his martial manner. He sat ramrod straight and bore himself with a dignity that, unlike his photo, demanded respect.

Who was he? None of us could figure it out. Was he a Chechen rebel, on his way home from some fund-raising mission to a Muslim fundamentalist group? Was he a pro-Russian Chechen returning from a secret peace-making conference? Everything we found out was communicated by means of mime, and Adam Mohammed Amin was a showman. He did a very good Grozny, graphically displaying its ruined flatness by chopping down imaginary buildings with a sideways motion of his hands. He even shot himself up with a make-believe machine gun, hanging his head and lolling his tongue out the side of his mouth. But as to whose side the General, as I began thinking of him, was actually on remained a mystery. No doubt it always will.

But not even sweet tea and a Chechen mime-show

could halt the onset of fatigue. I had to get some sleep. I tried lying down for a while, my head on my bag, at the back of the café. But there were rats running along a wooden cross-pole above me, and I was afraid one of them might fall. Finally I stumbled outside, telling my friends I would find them later, and plodded my way down to the water.

Once a sandy beach had stretched away from the harbour. Now it was covered in a thick layer of garbage and so filthy that the water beyond looked shockingly clean by comparison. I had never seen a sea as clear and limpid. But I cared nothing for any of it. I found a little depression in the sand that was out of the wind, laid my head on my bag again, and was instantly asleep.

I woke up hours later, hot and muzzy-headed. The sun was now well up in the sky and without moving I could tell that one side of my face had been burned bright red. My eyelids were stuck together. There were plastic bags and grease-stained chunks of styrofoam inches from my gaze when I finally opened them. I was grimy. I felt like a vagrant. Was this what the travelling life had come to – waking up sunburned on a filth-strewn beach in the middle of nowhere?

Suddenly I remembered the ferry. I sat up and looked at the harbour. A long line of transport trucks, their exhaust-stacks roaring, now waited before the harbour gates. Behind a concrete wall protecting warehouses and loading gantries I could see a ship with its own stacks pushing out heat. I scrambled to my feet. I was not going to be left as a cast-off beach-comber in this sorry place.

There was no one in the café. At the port's passenger gates hundreds of Egyptians were waiting in a queue that went far down the street and around the corner. I was about to head to the back of the line when I was grabbed by the arm.

It was Lotfi. 'Are you crazy?' he said in French, pulling me towards the front of the line. 'Come on. I've been looking all over for you.'

I objected, not wanting to jump ahead of passengers who'd been waiting patiently for hours.

Lotfi smiled and shook his head. 'These people are peasants. Believe me, it's not for you. You'll see.'

And I did see. Lotfi leading, we pushed our way through the gate and followed a single file of men that snaked its way between warehouses and into a vast, hangar-like building.

There were crowds of Egyptians already in there, divided into half a dozen lines inching towards glass-fronted immigration booths. At first I thought it was prayer-time; everyone was down on his knees. Then I saw that this was merely a crude form of crowd control – uniformed policemen stood beside the kneeling queues moving the men forward.

The immigration officers in the booths might have been processing cattle. They stamped documents and tossed them down with bored disdain. When a visa or work permit proved deficient wayfarers were sent off like bothersome flies, with a flick of the wrist. If they tried to argue their case they were hustled away by police and the next applicant called for. A holiday cruise this was not. But no one showed any upset at this treatment. It was the way things were done.

We cut in at the head of the line. There wasn't a squeak of protest behind us as we were stamped and waved through. 'Who are these people?' I asked Lotfi. 'Where are they going?' On the far side of a security barrier we found Jimmy and the General installed and waiting for us.

'I told you. They are nothing,' Lotfi shrugged as we sat down beside them on a bench in a crowded waiting area. 'They're migrant workers. They've been home visiting their villages in Egypt. Now they are returning to jobs in Jordan, Syria, the Emirates, Saudi Arabia. They are paid slave wages. But they are happy. At home they are paid nothing at all.'

The Egyptians spread themselves out on benches and floors, surrounded by mountains of baggage and hungry cats patrolling for hand-outs. In travel-stained *galabiyas* and head-cloths they were large, imposing men with work-thickened fingers and noses like large, blunt rudders. Their manners were rough. They stuffed their mouths with flat-bread and boiled eggs and raw onions. They wiped their moustaches on their greasy sleeves. They smoked endless cigarettes. They spat, chatted, laughed and guffawed. Were they happy, as Lotfi insisted they were? I had no idea, but not one of them showed the slightest impatience as, hours after its advertised sailing time, we continued to wait for our ferry.

When the time did come there was an almighty rush, hundreds of men all trying to pile up gangways at the same time. They swarmed over the boat, loud and anxious in their claims for this place or that. Our party of four found an awning-covered bench near the stern. But it did no good, for once everyone had settled down we waited another two hours moored fast to the quayside.

I couldn't say I minded staying close to dry land. The decks of the ferry seemed dangerously packed. The vessel appeared to have developed a pronounced list to starboard. 'Aqaba Ferry Disaster; Hundreds Drown' – it was the kind of bottom-of-the-inside-page headline you see all the time. But once we got underway I forgot all about danger. I had never seen a sea like this.

It was wholly different from that other sea lying only 150 miles away. The Mediterranean is just what it says it is, a middle sea. At certain times and places it can seem the loveliest thing on earth, but its beauty is the beauty of moderation, of balance and harmonious proportion. It is a sea built to the measure of man. The Gulf of Aqaba was nothing of the sort. It was a wholly immoderate thing. Never mind 'azure', 'cerulean', 'lapis' or any other brave attempt at hyperbole – its waters were impossibly blue. So were its mountains impossibly red, its air impossibly clear. So stark and alien was its splendour it hardly seemed to have a place for humanity at all.

Was that why the men aboard treated it with such contempt? They ignored the sea. Without the slightest glance at their surroundings they settled down once again to talk and smoking and food. Soon the decks were littered with eggshells and pumpkin seeds, banana skins and cigarette stubs. And when they finished they slung the remains of their meals overboard. For as far back as I could see we left in our wake a soggy record of our passage, plastic bags and floating bottles, bobbing soft-drink cans and empty Cleopatra packets. All were dispatched into this cleanest of seas with the blithest indifference.

And yet, for all that, there was a likable sociability about these travellers. They were a rag-tag tribe, but a tribe nonetheless. A few hours before, most of these men were strangers to each other. Now, cross-legged or stretched out on the deck together like old friends, they owned the boat. Their gregariousness, loud, emotional and excitable, took it over.

It was almost sunset when a thousand passports, collected on boarding, were redistributed with Jordanian entry stamps in them. A ship's officer stood on the poop deck as a stiff wind whipped the men's robes and the green, scimitar-emblazoned Saudi flag that flew from the stern. He shouted out names. The throng pressed in close to hear.

'Mohammed Badri Sulieman!' screamed the officer against the wind. There was a muffled response from somewhere in the rear of the crowd and a passport was passed overhead, from one hand to the next, until it reached its destination.

'Abdullah Ahmed Latif!'

'Mohammed El Shafie Mohammed!'

'Ali Zulficar Rafat!'

One after another the names were recited until all the passports were with their owners. By this point the sun was down over the Sinai desert and the wind had turned bitterly cold. Ahead we could see the lights of Aqaba. We'd be ashore in an hour, I told Lotfi. He nodded, but tentatively – no one, the gesture said, could predict rhyme or reason in the ferry's progress. Soon after the vessel slowed, and it was two more hours before we even entered port. Once docked, we spent another hour crushed in a corridor leading to the gangway.

I lost Lotfi, Jimmy and the General in the frantic rush that swept the boat when the doors were finally opened; although I waited some time in the Jordanian customs shed I never saw them again. I caught a taxi downtown and rented a $14 room in the Hotel Dweikh. Hungry for a bit of pampering, I took a lift to the eighth-floor bar of the Aquamarina, a plush resort-hotel overlooking the water. The beer was cold, the conversation restrained, and nobody spat peanut shells on the floor.

But for all the Saudi millionaires and well-heeled

Westerners who frequented Aqaba in the tourist season I had the feeling the city was rather a dull place. It seemed too clean and empty after Alexandria, too well run and predictable after the ferry. The Hotel Dweikh, though, had a surprise reserved for me. Fast asleep an hour after turning in, I crashed to the floor when the box-frame on which the mattress and springs of my bed was resting gave way.

I didn't move, but stayed there on the floor until the next morning. I was too tired to bother trying to fix anything. Besides, even the floor was a lot more comfortable and reassuring than the place I'd been dreaming about. In my sleep I was still lying in the burning sun on a flotsam-covered beach somewhere on the Gulf of Aqaba. Happily, the travelling life hadn't come to that yet.

Two

Does the Mediterranean Sea, as so many of its admirers claim, really have a beneficent and spirit-raising effect on its inhabitants? Does it moderate the temper, soothe the troubled soul and provide *allégresse*, that little bit of lift which makes all the difference in life? A couple of days later I was inclined to believe that it does. After months spent in the company of lively Alexandrians, Damascus seemed a dour and unyielding sort of place.

The bus connections had been good and I arrived in the Syrian capital just eight hours after leaving Aqaba. Not even the border crossing from Jordan, often a lengthy ordeal, had taken much time.

Syrian customs officers had begun a thorough search of the bus. I supposed they were looking for arms or drugs. They seemed particularly interested in a small refrigerator, a piece of equipment much valued by thirsty travellers in the Syrian summer heat, bolted over the bus's right rear wheel well. Having detached it from its base to see what might lie below, they spent most of their time lying prone on the floor, cursing and trying to locate the screws they'd lost somewhere down inside the bus's innards. By the time they'd got the thing more or less reattached they were so fed up that the rest of the procedure was perfunctory and we were soon on our way. There might have been five kilos of heroin and a dozen assault rifles sitting on the racks above our heads. It was reassuring to see that Syrian officialdom, with such a reputation for repressive efficiency, could be just as inept as any other officialdom.

In Damascus I inspected half a dozen small hotels. Without the world knocking at its door Damascus didn't have a vast range of choice in accommodation. It was either one of a couple of luxury hotels – against my principles on this non-touristic tour of the Mediterranean – or any of a large number of cheapies.

If the hot-water supply at the Candles Hotel was limited to a couple of hours a day the sheets were at least laundered and the blankets unstained. Nor were there any of those flimsy plastic bathroom slippers that the really squalid places laid on in lieu of occasionally cleaning the floor. I think it was the absence of the slippers, plus the nearby presence of the Hijaz railway station, that tipped the scales in favour of the Candles.

The station lay just across Hijaz Square, and compared with the grey, grim, poured-concrete constructions that made up much of modern Damascus it was a handsome building. But it wasn't just the look of the place. The truth is that for most of my life I've been a sucker for Lawrence of Arabia. As a twelve-year-old I'd tried Lawrence's *Seven Pillars of Wisdom* and found it an obscure and baffling read. I still do. But sitting in a darkened cinema a few years later I watched Peter O'Toole gliding about the desert in flowing white robes, his burning blue eyes half-mad. At the time I couldn't imagine Hollywood getting any better, and I still can't.

As Lawrenciana goes, the Hijaz railway is vital. Begun by the Ottomans in 1907, it was built ostensibly to ferry Muslim pilgrims on their way to Mecca down the Arabian Peninsula to the city of Medina. Its strategic military value became apparent in 1917, however, when Lawrence began blowing up trains to disrupt Turkish troop movements. As a rail terminus today the station is anything but vital – beneath its decorated ceiling and upper-floor gallery I gazed at architects' scale-models, plans for yet one more modern concrete complex into which the disused station was to be incorporated. But it made no difference – every time I passed the antique steam locomotive that stood on the square near the station doors I half expected to find it lying wrecked and smoking in the wake of a daring daylight raid.

Perhaps I didn't have to look very much further than the Hijaz station to trace the source of Damascene gloominess. Lawrence was not the first to have marched into the city at the head of triumphant warriors. Damascus lies only fifty miles from the Mediterranean, but it is blocked from the sea by the 6,000-foot-high Anti-Lebanon mountains. Sea trade has never been the city's *raison d'être*; instead it has traditionally straddled the inland routes leading from the Asian interior, and grown rich by controlling them. Sitting out on a broad, inhospitable plain, it has also been the target of enemies seeking the same kind of control. The longest continuously inhabited city in the world, it has been rolled over by foreign armies countless times in the last 6,000 years.

Not entirely countless. As I sat on my bed one evening waiting for nine o'clock – an odd hour for the hot water to come on, but better than nothing – I took my guidebook and made a quick tally of the various invaders and occupiers of Syria.

My list was partial, for I only began in the year 2334 BC. But it read like this – at various times Damascus had been taken over by: 1) the Mesopotamian Akkadians; 2) the Egyptians under Thutmose I; 3) the Mitanni Empire; 4) the Hittites; 5) the Phoenicians; 6) the Philistines; 7) the Aramaeans; 8) the Judeans; 9) the Assyrians under Sargon II; 10) the Babylonians under Nebuchadnezzar; 11) the Achaemenids; 12) the Greeks under Alexander the Great; 13) the Seleucids; 14) the Romans under Pompey; 15) the Persian Sassanids; 16) the Arabs; 17) the Cairene Fatamid dynasty; 18) the Crusaders; 19) the Mongols; 20) the Ottoman Turks; 21) the Egyptians, again, under a son of Mohammed Ali; 22) the Hashemite ruler Faisal, aided by Lawrence; 23) the French under League of Nations mandate; 24) the Egyptians for a fourth time, as senior partner in a short-lived United Arab Republic.

Well there you go, I thought as I heard the hot-water pipes finally rumble and gush – if you'd been knocked around by various foreigners a couple of dozen times even before the local Ba'ath party installed its less-than-benevolent regime, you too might just be the slightest bit hesitant in the *joie-de-vivre* department.

But there could be no doubt that Damascus, despite the torchings, razings and regime-changes, had over time continued to maintain control of the trade and caravan routes. It is a city of old-fashioned merchants and traders still. Not far past the Hijaz station new

Damascus suddenly vanished and motorised traffic disappeared. On the far side of a high surrounding ring of stone walls lay old Damascus. In its warren of streets, change, if it is takes place at all, is measured in centuries.

I hesitated on the morning I stood before its main gate and the high, vaulted arcade of the Souq al-Hamidiyya. Having taken a great dog-leg around Israel, I was anxious to get back to where, on this trip anyway, I belonged – the coast. My next stop was Latakia, Syria's biggest seaport. But I found it hard to side-step an ancient capital where so much of the eastern Mediterranean's fate was decided, and where so many of its actors now lie buried. This was the kind of place that could hold you back for days.

I plunged on in. The souq was cavernous, a long, busy, stone-flagged market dimly lit by shafts of sunlight penetrating the iron-roofed vault above. It was as I feared – behind the walls of Damascus sat an entire medieval Islamic world, much of it still intact and alive.

I wandered in the vast white marble courtyard of the Umayyad mosque, in the 8th century the very centre of the Islamic world. I visited the tomb of Saladin, the warrior whose capture of Jerusalem in the 12th century brought down the wrath of the Third Crusade. I watched an old woman on her knees, weeping in adoration before the mausoleum of another famous warrior, the Mamluke Sultan Beybars – he'd swept Christians from Antioch, burning it and them to the ground in the process. One sepulchre I stood in front of was said to hold the head of John the Baptist, a prophet to Islam as well as to Christianity. A second was purported to hold an even more celebrated head, that of Hussein, the assassinated grandson of Mohammed and the founder of Shi'ism. What happened centuries ago might have happened yesterday. Wherever I went in the old city I came across the same thing, people prostrated before the tombs of long-gone saints and warriors, kissing framed portraits and rubbing silver grillwork as if touch alone would bestow the departed one's blessing.

Growing weary of medieval martyrs I took myself

off to Bakdash, a venerable, century-old pudding shop. But here, too, the citizens of Damascus maintained their sombre alliance with the past. Bakdash made and served 3,000 bowls of pudding a day, but it would have no truck with modern efficiencies of any kind. I watched mesmerised as a cook poured milky-white custard from a large, spouted pail into endless rows of bowls. They filled at the precise rate of one bowl every second and a half.

'No machine can do better,' the man behind the cash register told me soberly as I spooned up my own pistachio-sprinkled pudding. 'He hasn't spilled a drop in thirteen years. Not one drop.'

There was something of this same methodical and unchanging traditionalism in every shop in the old city. It didn't matter if it was a boy turning chess pieces on a pedal-driven lathe, a tailor sewing sequins on a belly dancer's dress, or a brassmith working the bellows of his charcoal furnace. It wasn't just a matter of doing things in the old way. Damascenes appeared constrained, prevented from the possibility of doing new things in new ways. They seemed stuck in the past, cut off from the rest of the world's modernity. Even their cars were outdated. Sometimes a shiny big Mercedes with Lebanese plates – new money from a revived Beirut – would come nosing slowly through the narrow streets. But more often it was fins and torpedo-bumpers, the dinosaur appendages of Lincolns and Chevys carefully conserved from another age.

What was holding the place back? What made its people so buttoned up, so lacking in ease and facility? It was a question I asked myself all afternoon.

It was after dark when I finally emerged from the old city through its Christian quarter. Behind me lay biblical Damascus – the 'Street called Straight' and the window where a fleeing Saint Paul had been lowered from the city walls in a basket. Every alley in the quarter had been decorated with Christian symbols – religious images hung on outdoor walls and small statues were affixed above doorways and in wall niches. Now, back in the new city again, the street hagiography changed. Instead of Christ figures and Virgin Marys, the icons paid homage to Syria's secular deities, the Assads.

They were everywhere. The country's leading family were sanctified in statuary, hoardings, banners, murals, framed photos, posters and paste-on transfers on the rear windows of family cars. Just as common as Bashar al-Assad was his dead father Hafez, the man from whom he'd inherited the presidency. Also in evidence was Bashar's elder brother, Basil. Groomed for the top post but killed in a road accident before he could take over, the favourite son looked positively sinister in his signature three-day beard and aviator's sunglasses. Perhaps it wasn't just the dark clouds of the past that lingered over the Syrian plain, I thought. The self-perpetuating Assads appeared to cast a long shadow across it, too.

That evening I wandered around cold, wind-blown streets looking for somewhere to eat. The city centre was deserted and, like the capital's hotels, there wasn't a great range of restaurants. They were either formal and overly elaborate or little more than take-out stands. But finally I stumbled across an establishment that looked cosy enough.

'Al-Rayees Restaurant (Ex Normandie)', said the

sign outside. Inside there was a vague remnant of French provincial atmosphere left behind from the days of the Mandate. It was all a little shopworn. There were chandeliers hanging from a high, dim ceiling. Floral wallpaper, yellowed and curling at the edges, covered the walls. On one side of the room hung a framed print of Millet's 'Les Faucheurs'; from the other glowed the enigmatic smile of La Joconde. Had the Normandie been aiming to create the fresh and carefree mood of an outdoor *ginguette*? In one corner artificial vines ran up and over a white wooden trellis. It was a contrivance that failed miserably in the restaurant's thick, stale fug of tobacco smoke.

But it wasn't the décor of the restaurant that really interested me. It was the clients. The room was crowded with diners, all of them men, and as far as I could see not one of them belonging to the present era.

If I had shown up at a 1950s convention of intellectuals, artists and academics I couldn't have felt more of an anachronism. Everyone was dressed in Western fashion, but they were the dated styles of half a century ago. There were men with trim moustaches, tweedy jackets and thick, horn-rimmed spectacles. There were men in baggy flannel suits. There was one man with pointed, waxed moustaches, a black Astrakhan hat and a cape thrown over his shoulders. Even the staff came from another age – they dressed in black suits and bow-ties, and looked more like diplomats than waiters. No one was under sixty.

And no one was less than half-sloshed. Although the tables were covered with plates of food, most of it was *mezze*, a side-show. The main events here were drink and conversation, and everyone was hard at it. When the patrons of the Al-Rayees (Ex Normandie) stopped talking to pour raki, there was barely room left in the glass to cloud it with ice and water.

I was shown to a table covered with a fresh white tablecloth and given an English menu. The prices were ridiculously cheap and the spelling approximate – items ranged in cost from a box of 'Papper Klinex' (20 cents) to a steak 'Chateau Brillaund' (less than $3). As I studied the menu I also studied the dozen or so Syrians sitting at a long table in front of me.

One of them caught my glance and lifted a glass; with a beckoning hand he invited me over. His name was Fateh Ayub, he told me in English, and he always met his friends here. Would I join them? He wouldn't take no for an answer. In a minute I was picking at *mezze* and knocking back raki with the rest of them.

'And what do you think of our restaurant?' Fateh asked me, waving at the smoky room as he refilled my glass. I replied that I liked it.

'I have lived in many countries in my life, and travelled all over the world,' he said. 'But this is still my favourite place. Of course it's unfashionable – that's why we come. The same group of people – painters and writers and bohemians – have been drinking here for thirty years. It's our retreat. Listen to the music. That's not a pop-song; it's classical – the Arab *oud*.'

I liked Fateh Ayub right away. He was the first Syrian I'd met, and not what I'd expected. He was friendly, generous, hospitable and, in a country out of touch with the rest of the world, pleased to meet a foreigner.

I told Fateh I was heading for Latakia, and then on

around the Mediterranean coast. Latakia is not a town of any great tourist value, but Fateh surprised me by approving of my destination and telling me what I'd been telling myself for weeks. In a fragmented world, he said, the Mediterranean has always been a place of contact and exchange – it has a lot of old lessons to teach.

Fateh was a painter and loved the traditional Arab arts. But nothing excited him more now than the creative possibilities of cyberspace. For it, too, was a place of contact and exchange. 'Imagine,' he said with delight, 'communicating your ideas to anyone you like, anywhere in the world, instantly. Is there anything as fantastic?'

We talked for a long time and drank more raki than we should have. But no matter how relaxed we became, I noticed, Fateh never came even close to mentioning politics, the Assads or the regime they directed. There was little mention of public life at all. It shouldn't have surprised me. There are at least eight internal security services in Syria, each with its own network of secret policemen. In such a state some subjects are simply taboo. Our table finally broke up around midnight. As I gazed around a roomful of inebriated men preparing to go home, I began to appreciate Fateh's views of the digital world. For most of us the internet has lost its lustre and become just another tool. But for people like these – men who in a different place and time would be deep in the debates of public life – there weren't a great number of consolations. Drink and the internet were two of them.

I had a sore head the next morning but there was no time even for coffee at the Damascus bus station. Two soldiers were searching passengers' baggage at a barrier at the station entrance. On the other side a tout took charge of me. Less than two minutes later I was in a departing bus and on my way to Latakia.

At the very back I found the last available seat and squeezed myself down beside a young man. He was large, strongly built and wore black. His hair was close-cropped, his nose prominent, and on his forehead was a fixed scowl. We said nothing for the first ten minutes. Then, as the city gave way to bleak, stony expanses of open country, he spoke.

'Have you telephone?' he asked without preamble, the accent thick and the words coming slowly.

'Yes, I have a telephone at home,' I answered.

'Have you ... car?' he said with the same pained deliberation.

'Yes, I have a car.'

'Have you ... house?'

'I have a house, too'

'Have you ... woman?'

The have-you questions continued in this same slow, uninterrupted fashion for some time. It began to dawn on me that my questioner wasn't in the least bit interested if I had a telephone or a woman or anything else. He was more interested in talking. He was practising his English.

The exercise became tedious and to stop it I began asking questions of my own. My travelling-companion's name was Samir. He was twenty-four years old. He'd been studying English for six months. He tried to watch movies in English – 'I like Jean-Claude van Damme; you like Jean-Claude van Damme?' – but they were difficult to understand. Talking to foreigners was better, but they were hard to find.

'My English very, very good, no?' Samir would ask me every couple of sentences. Yes, I would say, very good. But it wasn't. It was bloody awful, and I was beginning to resent the man's blunt insistence. Not only was he slow and plodding; he didn't seem to have the sense or manners to know when to let up. As I gazed out at a cold grey sky and the remains of winter snow capping the hills above the plain he launched into another exercise taken from his grammar classes. Have-you-been. Have-you-seen. He was no good at it, but was becoming demanding and dictatorial. He was asking questions and he wanted answers. Not even my turning my head away put him off.

Fifteen minutes later we were back to the original subject, telephones. Samir was showing me his new Nokia mobile, and on its screen was flipping through the pictures he'd taken with it.

'This my brother ... this my father house ... ' I was barely watching, by now thoroughly fed up. But then he said, 'This me,' and there was Samir posing, a uniformed thug with a pistol in his hand and Basil-style shades on his face, the scowl stronger than ever.

Samir was pleased to see he had my attention. He was a member of the presidential bodyguard, he told me, and served in Bashar Assad's official residence in Damascus. There was no fear of politics in this man, I could see. In no time Samir had launched himself into fulsome praise of the President and made ringing paeans to the greatness of the Syrian state and army. The more he talked the more swaggering he became. Samir hated the Yahoudis (the Jews). They had stolen the Golan from Syria. They had built a wall around al-Quds (Jerusalem). They killed babies in Falisteen (Palestine). Syria had many enemies. But he, Samir, was there to protect it. He may only have been a 24-year-old punk hoping a tough-guy demeanour would impress me. But it worked. I was impressed. Samir made me nervous.

On the other side of the city of Homs the bus pulled over in front of a highway restaurant.

'Come,' said Samir. I said I would stay on the bus. 'Come,' said Samir again, beckoning at me. 'It is not your decide. You are my country guest.'

Inside he told me to sit. I sat. He ordered kababs and salad for me, and after, coffee for both of us. 'Eat,' he said. In the middle of the meal he got up and paid for everything. This was bad. It put me under an obligation – I would have to go through more mindless talk in more execrable English. Samir had me, a captive conversationalist, and he knew it.

Not far past Homs we began a descent coastward through the stony hills of the Jebel Ansariyya. Very quickly the country changed. As we headed down the sky cleared and the air warmed, and suddenly I knew I was close to the Mediterranean again. There were trees in red blossom and yellow wildflowers on the grassy slopes. Lower down on a broad coastal strip there were fields already high with grain and long rows of plastic-covered hothouses growing tomatoes. Small coastal villages began appearing, the walls of their simple, cube-like houses glowing pink and ochre in the bright sun. Women and girls stood by the roadside, selling bright piles of citrus fruit – oranges, lemons and the largest grapefruits I had ever seen.

It was a happier landscape than the one we'd left behind. Even the people in it looked happier. Through the bus window I could see villagers relaxing in the spring sunshine, laughing, sharing stories as they walked by the road. There were buoyant spirits here. There was *allégresse* in abundance. My only trouble was that I wasn't all that happy myself.

As we rolled along Samir had been talking on his mobile phone. Now he turned to me. 'My sister,' he said. 'In Latakia. First I show you everything. And tonight big dinner. We eat her house.'

I saw catastrophe yawning before me. I was being turned into a pet foreigner. I'd known Samir was going to spend a few days off work with his sister and her family. Now he was going to show me off like a trophy. There would be a lengthy, ceremonial meal, more tough-guy posing, more mangled English exercises. I couldn't do it.

'Samir,' I said, 'it's not possible. I've travelled all the way from Cairo. I'm tired. I need sleep.' On and on I went, but Samir wasn't having it. He refused my refusal. His face went red. 'You will come,' he said,

'No questions.' He began bullying, his voice growing louder. Did I want him to lose face in front of his sister and her family? Was I rejecting Syrian hospitality? He left me in no doubt that I was doing him a grave dishonour.

The more Samir barked at me the more I was determined to resist him. And finally he gave up, sitting sullen and wounded. He wouldn't say another word. The passengers around us looked away, embarrassed.

When the bus arrived at the station on the outskirts of Latakia Samir stomped off, head down, without a word. I stood with my bag on the platform, undecided. Latakia was not a big place. What if I bumped into Samir in the next couple of days? By then he might have recovered his cool and press his invitation even harder. Worse, he might have decided I had insulted him unforgivably. Was I being paranoid, or was he the vengeful type, someone capable of getting me into some kind of trouble? I mulled it over. Five minutes later I jumped on the next bus to Aleppo, miles from the sea on the far side of the mountains. I was there by sunset.

Three

I skulked around the souqs of Aleppo for the next three or four days, not feeling very proud of myself. It wasn't just that I had run away from a bully. I was also missing out on Syria's largest, busiest port. More than that, just fifteen minutes up the coast from Latakia lay the dead city of Ugarit, the oldest maritime trading centre in the world. But the thought of that scowling, resentful young thug, elite member of the *Sirayat ad-Difa' 'an ath-Thawra* – the Brigades for the Defence of the Revolution – was enough to keep me a safe distance away.

There were a couple of compensations. One was old Aleppo, still intact and, if anything, an even more magnificent medieval city than Damascus. The other, next to the tyre bazaar in the new city, was the Backpackers' Hostel.

It had everything – satellite television news, an internet café, a library, music, cold beer, full guiding services and a terrace dormitory for $2 a night. The place was packed – the clientele were the kind of young, adventurous travellers who end up in destinations that regular tourists wouldn't dream of setting their big toes in.

I met Charlotte Holloway watching BBC World on the hostel's covered rooftop. Together we contemplated the latest rounds of violence in Gaza, Iraq, Lebanon and Afghanistan. When the news was over and someone flipped channels to a re-run of *Friends* we went out to a pastry shop.

Charlotte ordered in what sounded like fluent Arabic. I was suitably impressed, until two gigantic servings of baklava smothered in nuts and dripping syrup arrived.

'Oops,' she said. 'That happens. A quarter-kilo is the only measurement I know in Arabic, so I do tend to over-order. And that's two portions I asked for. It is quite a lot, isn't it? Sorry.'

Charlotte was not an Arabist at all. Neither was

she an over-eater; she was tall and slim and could eat as much as she liked. And so we set to work on a pound of sticky pastry, and as we did so she told me about her archaeology studies at Cambridge. Operating on a shoe-string budget, she was in the middle of researching a thesis – her specialisation was in pre-classical contacts between Greece and the rest of the ancient world. She had also done work in Egypt and Albania, and would be flying on to Greece in the next couple of days.

Her obvious passion for her subject intrigued me – she'd soon pushed her baklava away and was detailing the intricacies of research that bordered on the edges of pre-history. I told her about my own non-academic interest in the Mediterranean as a place of human exchange, and of some of the things I'd come across in Alexandria. She listened carefully, sometimes nodding. At others she shook her head in disagreement.

'You're too European in your ideas,' she told me. 'Of course connective ties have always held the Mediterranean together. But why should it have been just the Mediterranean? They may have been concentrated there, but the same kind of ties stretched much further and in all sorts of directions we're still discovering. To see them you don't have to look any further than Ugarit. The idea of East and West as separate and distinct places is a recent concept. It was convenient to the Europeans who invented it. In fact, trade and human contacts made a seamless, single entity of the globe a very long time ago. A World-Wide-Web has been with us for ages.'

Charlotte became even more animated when I told her about Samir and my scuttling out of Latakia.

'To hell with Samir! He's probably gone home now anyway,' she said. 'It doesn't matter if he hasn't. You must go back there. Latakia is a nice place, friendly, and quite unlike other Syrian cities. But it's Ugarit that you simply have to visit.'

'Why?' I said. I had a recurrent day-dream of being condemned by a people's revolutionary court to a life sentence of adult education with Samir.

'Well, two things, basically,' said Charlotte. 'First there's Ugarit's age. It was trading across the

Mediterranean about 4,000 years ago. That's a couple of thousand years before Alexandria even came into being. It provided timber to the Egyptian Pharaohs. It had links with Cyprus and Mesopotamia. It exported bronzework to the Minoans of Crete. It was the first city on the Mediterranean to trade internationally.'

Charlotte turned back to her baklava.

'And second?' I asked. I needed all the reasons I could find to venture back down to the coast.

'Second is the small matter of Ugarit coming up with the world's earliest alphabet. Up until then the only two known systems of written communication used pictograms. But Egyptian hieroglyphics and Mesopotamian cuneiform were terribly awkward – literally hundreds of symbols were used to represent a complete range of words. The Ugarites reduced their own language to just thirty symbols. The communications revolution began there – it was the very beginning of easily stored and retrieved information. The city recorded everything from balance-of-trade accounts to its religious philosophy. The Ugaritic alphabet was likely taken over and adapted by the

Greeks, making it the forerunner of modern European alphabets.'

'And the place itself?'

Charlotte only shrugged her shoulders. 'In some ways there isn't much to see at all. The site is quite degraded and there's not much more than foundations left. It's overgrown and poorly looked after. Oh yes, and one more thing. The sea has receded – Ugarit's a good way inland now. But go. You'll understand when you get there.'

It hardly sounded like a world-beating seaport. But I looked at Charlotte. If this woman could negotiate her way around the Middle East knowing only how to say 'quarter kilo' then I could face up to my own challenges. I decided I would be on the first morning bus to Latakia.

Charlotte was right. Latakia was quite unlike other Syrian towns. The port-city was a buzzy, busy place, and right away I got the feeling it was more outward-looking than the inland cities. Latakia was not just a centre of the Alawite faith, an offshoot of Shi'a Islam to which the Assad family belonged; between the two

World Wars it had been a French colonial port and was still home to a large Christian population. As if starved of outside contact, Latakians literally stopped foreigners on the street to talk to them. After a day in the place I began to breathe a little more easily. Of Samir there was no sign.

I took a room at the Hotel al-Atlal, down by the harbour. It was run by an elderly Christian Arab with thick glasses and caved-in cheeks. He spoke slowly but precisely, and seemed to have taken a lesson in condensation from Ugarit's alphabet makers – he had almost as few words in English as he had teeth, but with them seemed capable of saying anything he liked.

There was one thing, though, he couldn't explain to my satisfaction. Where, I wanted to know, was the sea? From the hotel door the street ran two short blocks to a high wall and stopped. Above it I could see the tops of dockside cranes and the superstructures of cargo ships. The wall ran hundreds of yards in either direction. From nowhere in the city centre could you get the slightest glimpse of the water. It seemed a deliberate provocation – the construction of Syria's largest container terminal smack in the middle of an urban seafront. The city was cut off from the very element that had given it purpose since Roman times.

But seaports are open places by their very nature, and for all its invisibility the Mediterranean continued to work its cosmopolitan spell on Latakia. If the idea was to bar Syria's maritime gateway from importing new or different ideas it didn't appear to have had much effect. Latakia was liberal and tolerant in its habits. I saw few headscarves in the city. There were broad European-style boulevards, Christian churches and a Greek Patriarchate, tree-shaded avenues with outdoor café terraces, busy streets lined with bars and restaurants.

It was at night that Latakia really came to life. Was there any other provincial city in the Arab Middle East where women were quite as liberated? I doubted it. In the 'American Quarter', an up-market entertainment area close to the hotel, the sidewalks were thick with young Arab women in jeans; in skirts and boots; even in short blouses that occasionally but perhaps not inadvertently exposed a bit of belly-button. Does that fail to sound terribly daring? In Aleppo there were whole streets of dim, rundown nightclubs, little more than sleazy fronts for brothels. Now that's un-daring. What was impressive about the American Quarter in Latakia was its innocuous, international youth-culture style, its complete vapidity. In the Syria of the Assads exposed belly-buttons, MTV and teenagers crowding together for beer and pizza took a certain leap of imagination.

It was about eleven o'clock on a balmy spring evening when I walked out of the Stop 5, having had my own beer and pizza. Seeing happy couples holding hands made me feel a little forlorn, so I hiked off to the city Post Office to phone home. The building was long closed, but there were small-time scalpers by the outdoor telephone booths there who for a price would sell you a phone card.

Buying the card was easy, but the machine was unfamiliar and I couldn't make the connection. I tried three or four times, and then a hand reached over my shoulder and replaced the receiver. It wasn't what I had feared, the nightmare reappearance of Samir. The man behind me was stocky, grizzled, in his mid-fifties, and he was able to offer me help in the language of my choice – he spoke fluent English, French, German and Greek.

Home seemed far away that evening, and after I finished my call I had no objection to a bit of company. My new acquaintance, too, seemed happy to talk, so we strolled together through near-deserted streets. He was from Latakia, but had only recently retired as a captain in the Syrian merchant marine. He was blunt, his language was salty, but there was something appealing in his direct, no-nonsense manner. He had seen most of the world, and with a little prompting on my part could string together anecdotes about any port between Hamburg and Darwin.

But as we walked towards the city's old Roman gateway I began to get a little concerned. The Captain kept returning to the subject of his own home-port, Latakia. And what he had to say about it was not the kind of thing anyone said publicly in Syria. It started out discreetly, but each observation only seemed to make the man more agitated and outspoken. It crossed my mind that he might be testing my own desire to bad-mouth the regime, but I said nothing to encourage him. In the end there was such bitterness in his voice that I didn't believe he was anything other than an ordinary man who needed to let off steam.

As the city's stone Roman gateway loomed in the dark the Captain was complaining about the kind of shipping permitted to put in at Latakia. 'There are no regular freighters in the port,' he said. 'There are no passenger ferries in the port. It's all bastard containers. They want to keep the bastard port closed and under control. They want to keep us closed and under control, too. All we can do is pick our noses and act like monkeys and cheer the President.'

This was pretty strong stuff, but the invective against the state, the Ba'ath party and the Assads only got stronger. By the time we'd passed the New Mosque it had become more personal too. 'Do you know why I hate my fucking country?' he asked. 'Because they put me into the army for six years. A complete waste

– six years! And now they have just put my son in the same damned army. I warned him to get out, but now it's too late. Do you think our wonderful army is any good no matter how many people they force into it? It's shit! Shit! Three weeks, I tell you! If we had to fight a day longer than three weeks the entire bastard army would collapse! I guarantee it!'

This kind of rant was all right out in dark and empty streets, but as we approached the centre again there were more open shops and more people. The Captain was so upset by this point he didn't seem to care if anyone was around or not. We came to the Saahat al-Sheikh Daher, a principle city square overseen by a large statue of Hafez al-Assad standing on a high plinth. The Captain, ignoring late-night shoppers inspecting tomatoes and flipping through pirate CDs on sidewalk stands, pointed an accusing finger.

'Look at the old dinosaur,' he raged, his voice far too loud. 'Look up at Jesus Christ and pray. Bastard! Bastard! Baaastard …!'

I was thoroughly frightened by now, and even the

Captain seemed sobered by his last tirade. But some of the poison was out of his system, and he seemed calmer as we walked back towards the American Quarter.

'You understand, things are changing here fast,' he said in a quieter voice. 'People used to know nothing but what they were told. That's coming to an end. Now we have satellite TV. We have internet and e-mail and international telephone lines. People know what's going on. People know that the government speaks through this' – he pointed at his mouth – 'the way it speaks through this' – he pointed to his rear end. 'It cannot go on forever. I am sorry if I have disturbed you.'

We said goodnight and the Captain turned and walked away. The Stop 5 was close by, and still open. I needed a beer and a good dose of youth-culture vapidity. I'd had enough for one night.

Charlotte had been right about Latakia and she was right about Ugarit, too. It failed to overwhelm. When I arrived there the next afternoon there were no great ruins I could compare it to. It was not like the jungle pyramids of the Maya, the rock-carved tombs of Petra, or the ornate temple complexes of Ankor Wat. The old royal gateway into Ugarit looked like the outlet of a large city storm drain.

The whole place, in fact, reminded me of a vast, abandoned water-treatment plant. For the ancient Ugarites water was a vital element in all-important funerary rites, so the notion was not all that far-fetched — the place was a slough of wells, cisterns, stone-cut troughs, ditches, channels and subterranean conduits. Ugarit's engineers must have known a thing or two about hydrology, for the city, or what was left of it, sat on a little tableland elevated well above the surrounding country. Spread out below were the signs and sounds of more recent civilisation: neatly kept orange groves and vegetable plots, stands of dark cypress trees, white-washed, cube-like villages from which rose Arab music and the crowing of cocks. But Ugarit itself was anything but neatly kept. Its water works and foundations, its scattered stone blocks and the rubble of its once-great buildings were mostly hidden. They lay in a carpet of spring growth – spindly weeds, rich green grass and clusters of tiny wildflowers that waved in the breeze blowing off the sea. Ugarit was a place of serene and peaceful abandonment.

Apart from a gate-keeper who sold me a ticket there was no one about. I walked through the court-yards, halls and storerooms of the site's best preserved remains, its eighty-room royal palace. I strolled the ill-defined streets of its aristocratic quarter – like decayed teeth, its walls and houses had long ago crumbled to worn stumps. I jumped ditches, descended stairs into dank underground tombs and peered into dark cisterns. Behind the house of Rap'anu, where the first Ugaritic-inscribed tablets were discovered, I met a crippled hunter. Dressed in jeans and a ragged military tunic, he stood perched on crutches over a burrow-hole with a shotgun held awkwardly in his arms. Ugarit was the best place around for rabbits, he told me.

Finally, after a couple of hours of wandering over vast acres of ruins I came to rest at Ugarit's highest point, the city's sacred acropolis. In the temple of Baal

I found a low wall with a view, and sat down on it. Late afternoon sun was streaming almost horizontally into the dead city. It lit up rough swathes of green grass, caught the tiny filaments on weed-stems and turned them incandescent, illuminated miniature clouds of gnats hovering low over fresh pats of cow dung.

More than 3,000 years ago ships bringing cargoes from across the sea used to drop anchor just below Ugarit's royal gate. Now I could see the seashore glinting through a distant curtain of cypress trees – it looked to be a fifteen-minute walk away. After a while I heard mooing and saw a cow passing through the ruins of the temple. It was being driven home by a man and his two small children, and when they came abreast of me they stopped. Ugarit was even better for cattle than for rabbits – the man, who introduced himself as Ahmad, said he grazed his milk cow here every day.

Ahmad wore a sky-blue New York Rangers jacket, but he'd never been further than Latakia. Of course he knew all about this place and what it used to be, he told me. This was where civilisation began. 'Every man has two homes:' he said in a soft voice, '… where he lives now, and his first home, Syria.'

I wasn't sure, in terms of strict anthropological descent, that he was entirely right, but I did understand what he meant. And as if perhaps I hadn't, Ahmad went on to tell me that the whole planet's population was related. We all had common origins. 'That is why I am learning English,' he said. 'It is the language of world communication. With it I can share with everyone else. It is the best thing today.'

I couldn't help thinking of another, less globally-minded Syrian I had met who was also learning English. This was an astounding assertion coming from a poor cowherd wandering around a forgotten port stranded high and dry a mile from the sea. Ahmad, despite present circumstances – his cow, these ruins, his morally bankrupt leaders and wayward nation – had kept faith with the ethos of an old city. I was glad we'd bumped into each other. When Charlotte Holloway told me I would understand why Ugarit was important I hadn't been convinced. Finally I was. Even here, even now, old cosmopolitan ways had left their mark.

I watched Ahmad as he headed off to his village. Was he right? Would he ever belong to a larger world? Behind him the setting sun was reflected in the Mediterranean like a broad, bright roadway. The sea wasn't likely to return to Ugarit in the near future. But perhaps one day soon, not far down the coast, it might make a reappearance in Latakia.

Four

On the bus from Antakya to Adana cups of complimentary tea and coffee were handed out. The attendant who served them, a man in a spotless white shirt and black tie, behaved like a doctor about to conduct an intimate medical examination. Before making the rounds with his tray he carefully rolled up his sleeves, pulled on a pair of disposable gloves, and proceeded to handle plastic stir-sticks as if they were the latest in sterilised biopsy swabs.

I'm not saying this little demonstration was a sign of any great hygienic merit. When we stopped in Iskenderun to pick up more passengers the same man stood on the steps of the bus, studiously worked up a gob of phlegm and hawked it out onto the street. Above all, the gloves were a symbol of intent. For anyone who'd just crossed the Syrian border this felt like a get-ahead kind of place. Turkey had things on its mind and modernity, theoretically of the germ-free kind, was obviously one of them.

Coming over the high coastal pass separating the two countries the first Turk I'd seen was a peasant woman in baggy flowered pants hoeing a field. The next was a man in a flat cap and ancient suit, riding a donkey through a fruit-orchard carpeted in white spring blossoms. You couldn't help thinking in brochure-speak. It was quaint and it was colourful. It was timeless and unspoiled. And it all disappeared as soon as we got to the plain below. From Antakya onwards there wasn't much room for quaintness – it only got in the way of a busy, headlong rush of energy of a kind I hadn't felt in months.

Where exactly that rush was leading I couldn't say. Nor, I am pretty certain, could the other passengers sipping from their styrofoam cups. But it felt familiar. As the bus trundled along there was one franchise, one dealership, one assembly plant after another. There were Mitsubishi billboards, neon-lit Goodyear signs, yellow Opel banners flapping overhead in car-filled lots. Not only were they written in a non-Arabic script that I could read; I could understand them as well. They were telling me I had left a land arrested by sclerotic dictatorship and was back in the rough-and-tumble of a modern consumer society. Antioch, Tarsus, Seleucia … long ago the towns along these shores had been the stamping grounds of New Testament evangelicals caught in a fever of religious conversion. The Turkish Mediterranean coast should have felt ancient, exotic and biblical. But it didn't. After Syria it felt close to home.

I wasn't really convinced that I had driven into a horn-of-plenty – there were too many conflicting images lying just behind the billboards of mousta-chioed Turks driving new cars. On the far side of the Taurus Mountains, the steep range running behind the coast, I knew village Anatolia resembled Afghanistan more than it did any place in the West. Turkey was an old, poor place catapulting itself into the future. At one bus station I watched a whiskery country Turk in a ragged woollen hat abruptly hunker down on the platform, his knees to his chest, his posterior poised a couple of inches above the ground. He looked like he was preparing to answer a call of nature. Instead he settled down to take an incoming call on his cell-phone.

But as we travelled along there could be no doubting one source of a vigour that was contagious even through bus windows. Along with rough-and-tumble capitalism came free-wheeling politics. I had stumbled into the middle of a Turkish election campaign.

The city streets we drove through were a sea of banners hanging from buildings, lampposts and overpasses. There were plenty of star-and-crescent Turkish flags. But most carried the symbols of the country's political parties: the light-bulb of the AKP; the radiating arrows of the CHP; the dove of the DSP; the horse of the DYP. I counted more than a dozen different party flags. Outside campaign headquarters on the main road in each town there were milling crowds and impassioned speeches over fuzzy mega-phones. In suburban streets young men waving flags roared through traffic on motor-scooters. Even out in the countryside party militants were doing their best to rally the farming faithful – in the middle of nowhere we came across a campaign-parade of muddy-wheeled tractors stretching down the road and decorated with ribbons in party colours.

'Look, a rally for the Justice and Development Party,' the man in the seat next to me said as, pulling into the coastal city of Adana, we saw a crowd of long-coated, headscarved supporters gathering beneath a roadside marquee. 'The day after tomorrow there is a big election.' We rolled past the cheering throng, faces flushed and pink in their dark scarves, waiting to hear their candidate speak. 'Turkish women take their politics seriously.'

To me it was all fresh air – I had never seen such a strong contrast in neighbouring countries. All Turkey, left and right, Islamic and secular, was in a fever. And these were only municipal elections, a battle for control of towns and cities across the country. Before the bus arrived I made a change of plans.

I'd been intending to travel west along the

Turkish Mediterranean, following the coast to the Aegean port-city of Izmir. But the sight of the great landmass of Asia Minor rising behind the shoreline made me restless. How far into the hills did the sea's sway extend, I wondered – did 'Mediterraneanness' spread right across Anatolia? Were inland Turks very different from coastal Turks? Now this election campaign decided it. I would watch the last day of campaigning in the Turkish capital and be in Izmir the following day for the vote. As we rolled into Adana I consulted my guidebook. It looked possible. I would head inland by road to Ankara. And then, with a little luck and a free berth, the Blue Train – one of the country's top expresses – would whisk me overnight to Izmir. At the terminal I stepped off one bus and straight onto another.

It was easy, for in Turkey all roads lead to Ankara. Once, when all roads led instead to the Sublime Porte, seat of imperial rule in Istanbul, Ankara was a remote town lost on the high, arid steppes of Anatolia – then it was called Angora, and known only for a local species of fine-haired goat. Today it is the beating heart of the country, the seat of republican power, and the hub from which a strong guiding authority radiates out to direct the lives of seventy million Turks.

All roads may lead to Ankara, but Ankara buses don't. They stop a little short, and deposit passengers in a brand new bus terminal that sits miles from anywhere. It was so modern and vast it looked more like a major air terminal. It had an air terminal's milling confusion, too, and could have done with a little strong guiding authority itself. I couldn't get anyone to direct me at all, and it was well after midnight before I hunted down transport into town.

It doesn't really matter, though, what time you arrive in the city. Ankara announces itself as a place of serious intent at any hour. Even in the dark it *felt* like a capital city. It had weight and dignity. It had gravitas. It had more broad marble steps leading up to more monolithic institutions than I'd seen since I'd toured Washington D.C.

The shuttle bus cruised stately six-lane boulevards, stopping here and there to drop off passengers. One great bureaucratic complex after another drifted past in the night. Ministries, state buildings, administrative headquarters – all had grand facades, high, ceremonial doorways and – at one o'clock in the morning, anyway – a forbidding look. Official Ankara is built to make you feel small, and it does.

By the time the bus reached unofficial Ankara, the older, less opulent part of the city centre known as Ulus, I was the only passenger left. By now I had learned that travelling with an eleven-year-old guidebook to Turkey was not a wise idea – the country was changing too fast. But nothing had led me to expect the seedy doss-house the Lâle Palas turned out to be.

'The Lâle is a bit of old Ankara,' my dog-eared volume warmly enthused, 'with its marble and brass trim, faded grace and quiet welcome.' Since then the Lâle had acquired a dodgy nightclub with a couple of nasty-looking bouncers standing out front. When I found my way round to reception the welcome was all too quiet – it took me ten minutes to ferret out the night clerk, fast asleep in a room down the hall. Of marble and brass trim there wasn't a glimmer, but maybe that was because the whole place lay in the kind of eternal twilight that only 25-watt light bulbs can produce. All in all I could have done with a bit less of old Ankara, but it was too late and I was too tired to start looking elsewhere.

The first room the clerk showed me sat directly above the nightclub. The floor trembled and panes of glass in the windows vibrated. It was too loud to talk. I pointed upwards, and we tromped up four floors to the other side of the building.

The second room seemed all right. It was tiny. It held just four items – a bed, a bedside table, a cold-water sink and a telephone so ancient it appeared to be made of bakelite. More old Ankara. I dumped my bag, reducing the available floor space by half, and said good night to the clerk. It was only when I closed the door that I realised there was a fifth element, per-nicious, invisible and inescapable, occupying the room – the smell of old cigarette smoke.

Turks, of course, are heroic smokers – if you can't get used to it you might as well leave the country. Had I complained the night clerk would only have looked at me mystified. But I'd never experienced stale tobacco like this before. The stinking pillow and blankets were the least of it. Uncounted generations of Turks had exhaled so much smoke into the room that it had become an integral part of its construction – it had condensed into a patina on the ceiling, been absorbed into the walls and impregnated the floor. In three minutes my own skin seemed to be exuding the same residue. Sleeping in the Lâle Palas was like sleeping in an ashtray.

I opened the window wide but it didn't change much. It only let in the blare of the constant radio-traffic from the all-night taxi stand below. Nor was I any happier when I got into bed. The bottom of the sheet ended halfway down my calf and the springs were so badly bowed my bottom was a foot lower than my head and feet. I spent a restless few hours tossing and turning, and checked out early reeking like a Balkan Sobranie.

A hard, cutting wind was blowing up Atatürk Bulvari, the capital's main boulevard, and looked like it had been doing so for some time – the electoral banners and flags stretching across the street had been whipped to tatters. The morning was dark and overcast. Down on the Mediterranean the coast was green, the spring season full-blown. But here, almost 3,000 feet up on the Anatolian plateau, the city was still in the dead grip of winter. The trees on the sidewalks remained leafless and in the parks the grass was the colour of dishwater.

The few people out in the street at this early hour looked wan and washed-out too. Their coats were buttoned high and their faces were pinched as they leaned grimly into the sharp wind. There didn't seem to be anything Mediterranean about them. When Mediterraneans cross the street against traffic lights they dodge cars with careless insouciance. Here citizens didn't even try crossing the street against the lights. In fact I'd never come across a place that militated quite as actively against citizen-insouciance as Ankara.

When the traffic lights were red there was a visual display that gave pedestrians a second-by-second countdown of the waiting time remaining. When the lights turned green they showed a little electron-ically-animated figure ambling along; as pedestrian crossing time began to run out there was a sudden loud beeping and the little figure on the display broke into the energetic gate of a race walker.

'Marvellous', one might say, impressed with Turkish ingenuity and concern for traffic safety. But there is nothing like such devices for ratcheting up the general urban anxiety level in a place. Personally I'd rather see a few accidents. It might have been my own less-than-charmed mood after a night in the Lâle Palas, but I doubted it. Ankara that morning was a bleak city. The carefree *joie-de-vivre* of the Mediterra-nean does not penetrate to the heart of Anatolia.

Cold and shivering, I was one of the first visitors to Anit Kabir that day. The most austere and formal monument in a city of monuments, it sits on a low hill overlooking the city some way from the centre. But it was going to take more than a long trudge into a bone-cutting wind to stop me visiting the mausoleum of the greatest of all Turkish patriots. For here lay the man who had initiated the country's passion for secular republican democracy – Atatürk, father of the Turks.

The moment you set foot in the park that surrounds Anit Kabir you realise are on hallowed ground. Turks on the whole are an easy-going people, but one thing they will not tolerate: they might criticise his ideology or the acts committed in his name, but no one shows disrespect to Atatürk himself.

It was little wonder, then, that visitors accepted the admonishments of guards standing on the stone-flagged esplanade leading to the mausoleum. Asking Turks to put out cigarettes anywhere else is like asking them to amputate a limb. But here they meekly obeyed. Then they passed into a vast colonnaded courtyard overseen by an honour guard frozen to attention. Dominating everything was a national flag of a size you only usually see flying over US shopping malls.

Inside high bronze doors the atmosphere was more reverential still. There were glossy marble floors, more guards and the kind of brass rope-stands and red velvet cords you get at the Cannes Film

Festival. Visitors circulated clockwise, speaking in stagy whispers employed only for dramatic occasions. Atatürk's cenotaph, too, was exaggerated. His remains were actually buried in a smaller crypt below, but the focus of attention was a sarcophagus-like mass of carved and polished red marble. Twenty feet long, five feet wide and six feet high, it was built, like everything else to do with the man, on a larger-than-life scale.

The mausoleum left me cold; it was too grandiose and monumental to be appealing. Far more attractive, in a vast underground complex beneath the courtyard, was a stupendous museum collection of Atatürkana. Not only was there ample explanation of the historical context in which Mustafa Kemal, Ottoman general turned revolutionary nationalist, oversaw the birth of the nation. Here in room after room devoted to the man who incarnated the republic were ordinary possessions transformed into national icons. One of each was not enough. I counted a dozen walking sticks, five riding crops, half a dozen pocket-watches, nineteen cigarette cases, eleven cigarette holders, seven wallets, five notebooks, six pens, eight straight razors and Atatürk's personal rowing machine. That's not forgetting, of course, an extensive collection of fashionable Western formal wear – Atatürk was a snappy dresser – and the great man's dog, Foks, stuffed and mounted. I left feeling I knew as much about the father of the Turk's taste in smoking accessories and canine companions as I needed to.

No one down in the streets of Ankara, though, could doubt the seriousness of the man's legacy. In other Muslim countries to the north, south and east, other reformers had also single-handedly bent their nations to their will. But none of the Nassers, the Assads, the Saddams, Sauds or Pahlavis had given their people the kind of material and social progress, the democratic traditions that Atatürk had. And eighty years later that legacy was still being tested every day.

When I emerged from Anit Kabir early that afternoon there was just as much snow on the hills surrounding Ankara as there had been that morning. But downtown the political atmosphere had heated up. The streets were now thick with people and competition for public attention was fierce. There were long parades, speeches on city squares, campaign buses broadcasting party messages through giant roof-mounted speakers. Pamphlet-distributors were collaring voters on every street-corner. In one park, where a small anarchist party was holding a rally, there were more policemen in riot gear than there were participants. I wandered around for a long time, drinking it all in. Election day in the West was never like this.

At Kisilay, in the heart of Ankara, a young woman waylaid me on the sidewalk. Zahira was dressed in jeans and wore her hair in a pony-tail down her back. She was studying political science and could have come from any university in any country in Europe. I wasn't Turkish and couldn't vote, I told her. It didn't matter, she said. She was happy to talk politics with anyone.

Zahira was campaigning for a small left-of-centre party. But she wasn't hopeful that socialism would sweep the polls in Ankara. The capital, she said, was a conservative place.

'I don't mean religiously conservative,' she added. 'Look around. You won't see many Islamic headscarves here – you'll only find them in the poor parts of town. But this is the heart of Turkey, the centre of power and politics and government. It's not like Istanbul or Izmir. It's far from foreign influences. It has no past but its republican nationalist past. Ankara doesn't look outward for new ideas – it looks to itself.'

As we were talking a car shot by, its horn blaring. A fist emerged from the passenger window and made a sign – to me the extended forefinger and pinky looked like the sign of the *cocu*, a gesture made all over southern Europe in ridicule of the cuckold. But here it meant something else.

'They don't like us,' said Zahira, frowning as she looked at the car disappearing down the street. 'They are supporters of the Nationalist Movement Party. They are on the extreme right and they make a lot of trouble.'

'And what's this?' I said, wiggling my two fingers.

'Don't do that!' Zahira said sharply, shaking her

head. 'It's very bad. Those are the ears of the wolf. In Turkish mythology the lone wolf is a very old and powerful symbol. He is a mystical creature who led the Turkish people over the steppe to their ancestral home. The extreme right thinks that Turks are better and smarter than anyone else. These people are not intelligent. They hate Kurds. They hate Europe. They believe in a pure Turkish race.'

It was not extremism, in fact, but a broad-based movement that was Zahira's real worry. AK, the Justice and Development Party, had moved away from its radical Islamist origins – it was now seen as a moderate political force with religious tendencies. If AK militants frowned on liquor and encouraged prayer that was all right. More important, the party delivered – it was serious about paved roads, running water, well-lit streets and affordable transport. No one could object to efficient garbage collection, Zahira admitted, and AK's pragmatism had swept it to national power in the last general elections. The left would just have to learn to be better garbage collectors themselves.

Socialists, Communists, Nationalists, Islamists, Liberal Democrats ... in all there were fifty-five parties contesting the elections and every one of them was out on the streets. It was a battle getting through dense crowds and back to the hotel to pick up my bag, then carry it, still reeking of smoke, to the Ankara railway station. I found the last carriage of Train 314, the express 18:10 Blue Train to Izmir, just four minutes before departure, and collapsed gratefully inside.

Five

Aboard the Blue Train, I had a two-berth compartment to myself and it was spotless. A uniformed steward knocked on the door and showed me how to fold the un-needed upper berth away. He also showed me a sink with hot and cold water, mirror and towel; a luggage rack; hooks to hang clothing on; a miniature fridge containing fruit juice and chocolate bars; a vent-control for fresh air; reading-light switches; a call-button for any hour of the day or night. Two carriages down, the steward told me, was the dining car – grilled lamb chops were being served even as we spoke. And if this sounds like a too-careful enumeration of what are really quite basic traveller's amenities, then all I can say is you've never stayed at the Lâle Palas Hotel.

I might as well have been floating on a cloud, and turned in early after dinner. All night long the Blue Train rattled and rolled, sometimes rushing, sometimes crawling cautiously ahead, sometimes lying-up silently as a goods train flew by in the opposite direction. I slept as one always sleeps on trains, intermittently. But I was happy anyway. I was closing in on Istanbul. Like a rail-carriage sliding in and out of sidings I slipped from one dream to another. I dreamed of Chechen generals in Sergeant Pepper uniforms, of scowling Samir in his sinister black security get-up, of Mustafa Kemal dancing like Fred Astaire in white tie and tails. And when I came to in the morning and raised the compartment's curtain I knew I was down off the Anatolian plateau.

The first thing I saw from the window was a yellow house in a field with two palm trees in front of it. The sun was shining and the leaves were back on the trees. It was warm outside. The Blue Train was too modern to have pull-down windows, but I would have opened them if I could, just for the smell of the air. Half an hour later, with the blue Aegean a ten-minute walk to the west, we were pulling into Izmir's Basmane Station.

I was tired of cheesy hotels and for once decided Mediterranean authenticity might be just as easily attained with a slightly higher level of comfort. Around the corner from the station I walked into the Hotel Baylan, a clean, pleasant place used by visiting businessmen. Dressed in suit, tie and crisp white shirt, Mr Ikbal Çelik, its cheerful general manager, offered me a glass of tea.

'Of course we have a room for you today,' he said. 'We even have a special reduction for you today. Because no one is working and no one is travelling. No one is doing anything but voting. The whole city is closed down.' Mr Çelik had a vigorous manner. 'You cannot buy a drink until eight o'clock this evening when polling stations close. You cannot carry a gun today, even if you have a licence for it. All you can do is vote.'

'Who is going to win?' I asked.

The manager needed no time to consider the question. 'In my heart I am Left.' He said it so proudly you could hear the capital L. 'But today the country is Right. AK will win.'

Like Zahira in faraway Ankara, Mr Çelik had to admit that AK, the party of moderate Islam, had brought efficient administration to Turkey. Nor were they any longer an extremist party; they were co-operating with the military, with business, with pro-Western parliamentarians,with the Kemalists. They were as interested in joining Europe as anyone else.

'The Kemalists?' I said.

'Yes. I am a Kemalist.' Mr Çelik sat up a little straighter, a little more officially in his chair. 'I vote for the CHP, the Republican People's Party, founded by Mustafa Kemal, Atatürk himself. It is secular and democratic and outward-looking ... like Atatürk himself,' he added.

'Will the AK win in Izmir as it's supposed to in Ankara?'

'That, most definitely not!' Mr Çelik said with alacrity. His mouth widened with a broad smile. 'Izmir is a progressive town. Ankara is a city of big politicians and big business. Izmir is a working-man's city, a place of industry and trade. We are too busy working here to spend time praying. We load and unload and assemble. We are a port – we do business with the whole world.'

Mr Çelik, with no clients to look after today, was enjoying himself. He took a sip of tea.

'We are international in mentality. When I was a child there was just one international trade fair in all Turkey. It was here, in Izmir. It was the time of the Cold War, but that didn't matter – the United States, the Soviet Union and every other country had trade stands and exhibitions. It was wonderful. I saw a model of the Apollo rocket. Very big. I even leaned over a railing and touched an American spacesuit, a real one. Do you think boys in Ankara could do that? Never!' said Mr Çelik. His eyes were bright with the memory.

'Now there are trade fairs everywhere,' he conceded. 'But Izmir is also the south-east head-quarters for NATO. Behind the Hilton Hotel, by the NATO commissary, there are shoeshine boys who speak the best English in the city. And trade is getting busier all the time. Our port isn't big enough anymore. Izmir doesn't look in, Izmir looks out.'

Izmir, seen through Mr Çelik's eyes, seemed to be following a general pattern in this part of the world – cosmopolitanism was a coastal affair. I went for a walk. I didn't need a drink and I didn't need a gun, but I could see that Mr Çelik was right – the city was shut down. It was so quiet that when I passed by the Hilton Hotel there wasn't a shoeshine boy in sight. But what surprised me even more was that for a Mediterranean town Izmir looked practically new. Just down the coast lay the ruins of Ephesus, one of the largest and best-preserved cities of the classical age. But here there was little that looked even a century old. Most of the city was made of concrete, and not very pretty. Why, I asked Mr Çelik when I returned to the Hotel Baylan and found him still sitting idly behind his reception desk drinking tea. Mr Çelik was not only an enthusiastic tea drinker and Kemalist and toucher of space suits, he was proud of his city's past as well. He ordered an extra glass for me and settled in to explain.

In 1920, he said, Turkey had collapsed and the Ottoman Empire was in ruins. With the end of the war the victorious Allied powers had agreed not just on the dismemberment of the empire that had allied itself with the Germans, they had planned a carve-up of Turkey itself. By treaty accord Thrace in western Turkey was to go to the Greeks. Italy was to inherit a large part of the Mediterranean shore. Britain and France, already granted control of Iraq and Syria, were awarded much of the southeast, minus a portion slated for a future Armenian state. The Russians were to be given a chunk of territory in the northeast. The Dardanelles and the Sea of Marmara were to be jointly administered by the Allies. Turkey was to be left a land-locked rump-state on the arid central steppes. The arrangement was regarded as nothing less than historic desserts, the fate awaiting a major European adversary for centuries.

One country had not even waited for the Treaty of Sèvres to be drawn up, said Mr Çelik. Was the hotel manager an amateur thespian as well? His face grew suddenly clouded, his gestures oversized and dramatic.

Already the year before Greece had embarked, with Allied blessings, on a military invasion of Turkey. The project was an old one – the Greeks had nurtured the *Megali Idea*, the Great Idea, ever since independence from the Ottomans in the 1830s. But their profound resentment went back a good deal further than that – what the Greeks wanted was in essence a refounding of ancient Greek Byzantium and its empire in Asia Minor.

They began, logically, said Mr Çelik, with Symrna, the ancient port-city that under the Turkish republic was to become Izmir. Whether Homer was a resident of Symrna, as tradition has it, remained unproven. Mr Çelik certainly believed he was. What was sure was that as long ago as the Homeric age Symrna was one of the most prosperous Greek colonies along the coast of Asia Minor. Later, as part of the Byzantine empire, it was one of the greatest of Mediterranean ports.

Symrna had retained its Western character even under the Turks. Less than a century after the Ottomans stormed Constantinople in 1453 Süleyman the Magnificent – a powerful but enlightened ruler, opined Mr

Çelik – granted François I of France Turkey's first commercial treaty. It gave foreign merchants the right to live and trade in Ottoman territory, and before long Smyrna was the most Western and cosmopolitan city in the Ottoman Empire. Home to tens of thousands of foreign sailors, merchants and diplomats, the city claimed more Jewish and Christian residents than it did Muslims. A dozen nationalities shared in its sophisticated society and the Greeks, of course themselves Mediterranean traders *par excellence*, were pre-eminent among them.

But in 1919 the Greeks were looking to claim more than Smyrna alone. With the Ottomans' Grand Armies destroyed and their imperial administration in tatters at the end of the World War, the Turks could offer little resistance. 'The Greek's big idea grew bigger every day,' said Mr Çelik, tension building in his voice. Soon they had taken the inland city of Bursa, and by September 1921 they were fighting on the outskirts of Ankara, the town declared Turkey's provisional capital by its desperate nationalist defenders.

Not only had Greece, a former Ottoman vassal,

taken Smyrna; now it had marched deep into the
Anatolian heartland as well. The shock of near-
annihilation served to revive a demoralised Turkish
people. 'It was then that Mustafa Kemal became a
great national leader,' enthused Mr Çelik, who in
telling his story seemed to undergo revival himself
– his face was bright and lively. Under the general's
direction the Turks reorganised and retaliated. In
bitter fighting the Greeks were halted, held, then
driven back. Their retreat became a rout. A year later,
with Turkish troops in hot pursuit, decimated Greek
forces were escaping from Symrna harbour by any
vessel they found afloat. In the process the ancient city
was destroyed, burned almost entirely to the ground.
But the day that Mustafa Kemal – by now Atatürk –
entered Izmir was the day he declared victory in the
Turkish War of Independence. Soon after he declared
the foundation of the new republic, too, and the
Allies, bowing before a *fait accompli*, acquiesced to a
renegotiation of Turkey's treaties.

And so Izmir, Mr Çelik beamed, became a symbol
of nationalist triumph born out of disaster. It showed

that, given the right leadership and the kind of patriotism it inspired, a nearly decimated Turkey could become a potent force. What Mr Çelik didn't say, proud Izmiri that he was, was that under nationalism's thrall even an old and cosmopolitan coastal city could be shown up by a raw, brash new rival far out on the plains of central Anatolia.

But Mediterranean cities, like the phoenix of classical myth, have a way of rising from their own ashes. Izmir might no longer be a great mix of races. As I discovered the next morning, though, it has become its busy, cosmopolitan self again.

I stopped off at the reception desk on the way out. Mr Çelik was no longer there. His place had been taken by a clerk who stood poring over a newspaper. An enormous, bald man who would have had trouble with an 18-inch collar, he looked like a Turkish tag-team wrestler. But like his boss Mr Çelik he was an old-style republican, a dyed-in-the-wool Kemalist.

He was both happy and sad. He turned the main page of the paper around on the counter to show me coloured maps and figures. AK Islamists had swept the country, winning more popular votes than the next three parties combined. They had taken Ankara and Istanbul with over half the ballot each. They had won three-quarters of the principle mayoral races. There was just one anomaly. The main opposition party, the Kemalist CHP, had easily won in Izmir. In fact all the eight cities won by the Kemalists were port-cities on the Aegean Sea.

'Why?' I asked.

The clerk spoke no English but understood the question. In answer he merely raised a large, horizontal palm high in the air, as if measuring the distance from the ground. '*Kultur Ege,*' he said, indicating the considerable height with his eyes. I spoke no Turkish, but understood the answer. 'We in the Aegean,' he was saying, 'are more sophisticated than the others – that's all there is to it.' The Turkish coast was a last hold-out of cosmopolitanism.

Leaving Mr Çelik's assistant glued to his newspaper, I walked through a busy bazaar area and emerged onto the waterfront at Konak Meydan, Government Square. Like Alexandria, Izmir sooner rather than later pulls its visitors down to the sea, and it, too, has its Corniche. It is called the Kordon, after another French word, and much of the city's lively outdoor life is concentrated there.

The Konak Meydan was as modern and unexceptional as any other part of the city. But the sea beside it was anything but unexceptional. At the far end of the square began a great, deep bay, with the heavily built-up hills of the city running steeply down to the water on all sides. Out there on a sparkling roadstead freighters rode at anchor, tugboats nosed about arriving ships and hooting ferries plied their way through traffic to the far side of the bay. I had no need to cross over to the suburb of Karşiyaka, but then I saw the *Kapitan Mustapha Güler*, a ninety-foot, double-decker ferry gleaming white in the sun and about to leave. I couldn't resist it. Running to the terminal to buy a token, I made it through the turnstiles and hopped aboard just as the ferry was pulling away.

The breeze out on the water was glorious, not sharp like the winds off the steppe but fresh and inviting, full of hints of distant places. From out here I could see not just the path to the open sea but the inner harbour at the end of the bay. It was a mass of wharves and cranes, tall gantries for hoisting containers, silos for grain and cement, dry docks for big-ship repair. The other passengers had seen it all before. Having made the commute a thousand times they read their papers or drowsed in the sun. But as the *Mustapha Güler* cautiously tacked its way across a busy flow of traffic I watched ships.

There was the *Apache* out of Valetta, escorted on its slow way out to sea by a patient tug. There, too, heading the other way, was the *Georgos I* from Latakia. We dodged ahead of the *Rafik*, a rusty little coastal steamer flying an Egyptian flag, and wisely awaited the passage of the *Salerno Express*, a giant container-carrier flying the Maltese cross from her stern.

There were other ships too far away for their names to be read, but as I stood by the rail peering out I noticed I was not the only passenger taking an interest. Sitting on the bench behind me was a small boy gazing out over the water and asking his father questions. There was a look on his face I had seen before. It showed the same curiosity, the same sense of intrigue with the unknown and faraway that I had seen in Ikbal Çelik's face when he described a now long-gone trade fair. The *Salerno Express* was hardly as impressive as an Apollo rocket. But of such contacts and curiosity are Mediterranean seaports made.

Twenty-four hours later, 150 miles to the north, I was looking at another sea and another port. The train trip from Izmir to the ferry-port of Bandirma on the Sea of Marmara had taken all day. I felt grimy and worn out. I was tired of trains, of buses, of hotels good and bad, of vast, unknown cities arrived at in the middle of the night. I'd been three weeks on the road, and was looking forward to settling down and not having to move at all. Istanbul lay just over the inland waters of the Sea of Marmara. Aboard a high-speed ferry, the *Turgut Ozal*, the crossing would take less than two hours.

I was looking forward to coming to a halt for another reason, too – I was growing lonely. Solitary travel is a process both sociable and isolating. Not far from the harbourside café I was sitting in I could see a phone-box, and decided to phone Jany at home.

I had kept in touch with her from Egypt, Jordan, Syria and Turkey, and I thought I knew pretty well what was going on. But with Jany you never knew exactly what was next. Like the sea coast I was following she was Mediterranean, and just as unpredictable. She was lively, mercurial, emotional, demonstrative and voluble. Voluble, especially, on the telephone, and now what she had to tell me ran us through three phone cards.

The long and the short of it was that Easter was coming up and with it a break for Jany from teaching. When I had set out for Alexandria after the New Year I'd had no idea where I would be for Easter. Now that I'd finished my swing through the Middle East, she suggested, she could join me for three weeks.

Wonderful, I said, Istanbul was still coolish, but free of the tourist crowds that would descend like Crusader armies later in the season.

'Istanbul wasn't exactly what I had in mind,' she told me from distant Aix-en-Provence, her voice loud and clear. Her voice was always loud and clear when she'd decided on a plan.

'I'd love to see Venice in the spring,' she said. 'We could meet there and then you could carry on eastward to Istanbul when I go back to teaching. You wouldn't miss an inch of the coast – you'd just be doing part of it the other way round.'

Most of my life had been the other way round since I'd met Jany, so I didn't see why it should be any different now. We talked a good deal more. But in the end I agreed, as Jany knew I would from the beginning, that I would fly out of Istanbul.

I boarded the *Turgut Ozal* in two minds. On one hand Istanbul, my goal for so long, was being snatched away. On the other I was feeling worn out and tired – the idea of a posh, pampered existence in one of Europe's most elegant cities rather appealed.

As we roared off across the water the sun sank, night fell, and the sea and sky outside the windows turned inky black. I was left with nothing to look at but ferry staff dishing out dinner in a brightly lit cafeteria. They wore little white sailors' uniforms with blue-trimmed caps and seahorses embroidered on their shirtfronts. They distributed clingfilm-wrapped sandwiches with efficiency, with panache and style even. But this was hardly the romantic sailing into Istanbul that I had imagined.

Nor was the landing itself. Instead of sailing up the Bosphorus and in under the harbour-lights of the Golden Horn, we berthed in a modern new ferry terminal miles to the west on the Marmara coast. The only lights I was going to see that evening were the runway lights of Atatürk International Airport. But it didn't matter. Venice, if half of what they said was true, was a city of some romance itself.

Six

We hopped a train from Mestre, and rode a clattering metal causeway out into the Venetian lagoon. Two miles off the Italian mainland, Jany and I emerged from the doors of the Stazione Ferroviaria Santa Lucia, a railway station among other railway stations. And from the top of its broad steps Venice, a city among other cities, was suddenly like nowhere in the world.

It was moving. Of course all cities move — constant, restless motion is their nature. But Venice was moving *up and down*. It bobbed. Even at this early hour the Grand Canal was heaving with traffic. Wherever we looked objects were rising and falling on the agitated liquid surface that bore them.

Other travellers, like we train-passengers about

to become boat-passengers, were pouring past us and down to the quay beside the water. But as generations of newcomers have done before, we stood wordless at the top of the steps, agog at life.

Commuter-crammed *vaporetti*, the city-buses of Venice, cut heavy, undulating swathes as they churned their way from one canal-side stop to the next. Show-off *motoscafi*, the immaculate launches that make up the city's snooty taxi fleet, cleaved faster, lighter trails over the water as they scooted wealthy patrons to suites at the Cipriani or the Danieli. A blue, square-ended garbage scow, its hydraulic claw poised above a heaped cargo of plastic bags, floundered slowly by. Improbably, it, too, managed to look like a superior kind of vessel.

There was every kind of craft dipping and dancing out there. There were vegetable barges bearing crates of bright tomatoes and shiny purple aubergines to market; post office boats carrying letters and parcels; raked-back, slate-grey pursuit vessels belonging to the *guardia di finanza*. There were the flame-red fire-boats of the *vigile del fuoco*; vintner's boats laden with crated bottles and plastic-covered demijohns of wine; laundry-boats picking up dirty sheets from one hotel after another.

Coming and going amidst these specialised craft was the *topo*, the hard-used, all-purpose delivery-vessel of Venice. I looked at the merchandise floating by on the battered decks of these Venetian work-horses – there were boxes of feather-light *biscotti*, half-ton office photocopy machines and just about every kind of cargo in between. And all of it was in motion, rocking up and down as boats criss-crossed paths out on the canal. Even unpropelled, inanimate objects like the floating *vaporetto* dock in front of us were semi-mobile – chained to the quay and staked between heavy wooden pilings, it couldn't help but jump and slew about as the wakes of passing craft fanned out to slap at the canal's banks.

I was mesmerised. The only other canals I knew were the three intersecting canals of Little Venice in London. Now I could see just how little they were. The Grand Canal alone was two miles long. Radiating out from it, capillaries in a giant circulation system feeding fresh tide-water into the city, were 176 other canals. Narrower but only slightly less grand, they made up a maze whose total length exceeded twenty-eight miles. There were no proper streets in Venice, but more than 3,000 twisting alleys and bridged passages wending their way beside and over the water. There were no cars, no wheeled vehicles apart from delivery trolleys, prams and shopping carts. On the other hand, Venice could claim some of the most splendid palazzi in the world. And just as attractive, as far as I was concerned, was its collection of boats – the city harboured an armada of the most exotic and unlikely watercraft in the world. Venice was a boatman's paradise.

Jany was as enchanted as I. But other, more practical matters now lay before us. Somewhere in Venice, down one of those canals, our own small, homey version of a palazzo lay waiting. Jany dragged me back into the station to a bank of public telephones, and for the next few minutes she was busy talking.

A brief word, for a moment, about my wife's

communications skills. Talk, for Jany, wasn't really a social skill at all – it was as necessary to life as breathing. If you stopped her conversing for very long you stopped her altogether. Nor was communication merely a vocal art; it was a visual activity as well. It involved her whole body, especially face and hands. I could follow Jany at fifty yards through a crowded street simply by watching for her hands. They were like restless birds attached to the end of her arms. In the event of a power black-out and complete darkness I wasn't sure Jany was capable of spoken exchange at all.

To a circumspect Anglo like me, such verbal conviviality was foreign – it was as good a symbol of Jany's thoroughly Mediterranean character as any. That she had become a language teacher was no accident – it gave her talents for communication the fullest scope possible. Her gift for sociability was operative in all places and at any time. On the bus, at the bank, in a supermarket check-out – in two seconds she'd fall into conversation with strangers, and strangers would soon become friends.

Planning for Venice had been no exception. Spending weeks in a hotel there, I knew, was going be near-unaffordable. Like its garbage scows, even modest hotels in Venice affect superior airs – they are happy to command some of the most inflated rates in Europe. I'd raked the internet and there appeared to be no other option.

Then Jany put more human skills to work. She taught Spanish at a *collège* in Aix-en-Provence, and had a network of teachers, teachers' friends and friends of teachers' friends that stretched from the Pyrenees to Andalusia. But she could just as easily follow other lines of communication extending in the opposite direction.

At a school in Marseilles Jany knew a teacher of Italian, who'd introduced her to an artist living in Montepulciano, who'd put her on to a Sicilian couple who'd moved to Venice and were on friendly terms with ... I won't bother continuing, but on it went, one link leading to another in a coil that wound its way up and down Italy, crossed the lagoon at the head of the Adriatic, and ended up in a small apartment by a minor canal on the eastern edge of the Venetian district of Cannaregio. Pinella, the apartment's owner, was visiting her mother in Ravenna for a few weeks. In the meantime it was ours. All we had to do was get in touch with Pinella's ex-husband, Caesar, an abstract painter and creator of fragile objects pressed from hand-made paper.

Such was the convoluted trail by which one telephone call and twenty minutes later we found ourselves standing on the *vaporetto*-landing at Ca' d'Oro, on the great S-bend of the Grand Canal in the heart of the city, eyes peeled for a man we'd never met before. Caesar, when he arrived, appeared every bit a bohemian artist of Venice, his fingers long and delicate, his goatee greying, his waistcoat vented and cut from elegant silk. So we weren't surprised, either, on being led through a labyrinth of narrow alleys, to find an apartment that looked every bit a bohemian apartment of Venice.

It was old, and reached by a worn flight of stone steps from a dim ground-floor hallway. Half a dozen umbrellas stood in a stand inside the door to the street. The hallway walls, in the baroque style called *scagliola*, were painted to imitate marble. Inside the apartment the ceiling was high and painted in geometrical patterns of sienna and dull mauve, old yellow and pale rose – colours so faded and obscured by time they now threatened to disappear altogether. In other rooms twisted wooden beams, dark with age, straggled across the ceiling. The floors, too, were ancient, a pressed assemblage of the tiny coloured pebbles, polished to a dull sheen, known as *terraza alla Veneziana.*

But it was the marriage of the traditional to the minimal that I enjoyed. The kitchen was all sleek design elements of burnished steel and the tropical hardwood floor in the bathroom reflected a rich halogen glow. The paintings on the wall were modern, and Caesar's own.

'Spaghetti,' said Jany after he'd closed the front door quietly behind him, leaving us alone in proprietal splendour. She was looking at a painting of long, wavy parallel strands scraped down to white canvas through dark paint.

'The Grand Canal and its lesser confluents,' she added, switching her gaze to another tableau of the same type, a single, broad wavy strand surrounded by a confusing trail of narrower ones. She may have been right, but I wouldn't have counted on it – she tended more towards the figurative than the abstract.

We didn't know where to look first.

We opened shutters in the rear bedrooms and gazed down onto a green garden, and in it a terracotta-tiled house whose walls radiated a patina of lush red. There was a tall magnolia tree on the lawn, a glistening bay laurel, stone benches, a trellised vine and singing birds. Best of all, when the windows swung open an odour of raisins and spices, cinnamon and warm pastry wafted into the rooms. Someone nearby was baking.

We unpacked – in my case, a bag you could take in the cabin of an aeroplane; in Jany's, a suitcase not much smaller than a steamer-trunk.

'Couldn't you have brought a little less?' I asked as I dragged it down the hall and into the bedroom. In a city without wheeled transport such luggage is inadvisable. But Jany seemed to have made her travel arrangements according to some bizarre law of inverse proportion.

'Well, I could have brought less if I'd had more time to pack,' she said as if it were the most obvious thing in the world. 'It's not what you take; it's what you have to decide what not to take that makes it difficult. I didn't have time.'

I said nothing more. For I had been around Jany long enough to know that there were differences between us, most of them having to do with two ways of looking at the world – one Anglo, the other Mediterranean – that were not worth debating. It was better to simply accept and adapt. Jany's peasant-farmer ancestors had accumulated and hung on to tiny plots of earth through the centuries – not a square inch was ever willingly given up. Did her Mediterranean world-view extend to the aggregation of baggage as well? I wasn't sure. All I knew was that often enough it took something less crucial than a Samsonite suitcase to provoke a clash of civilisations. So I kept my peace.

We put our things away. There were women's dresses hanging in an armoire, folded shirts in the drawers. Jany sniffed at soaps and toiletries in the bathroom. I inspected small bits of clay statuary and art books stacked on living room shelves. We poked at pots and pans in the kitchen. There were olives and apples, pecorino cheese and jars of jam in the refrigerator. On the counter beside it was a half-finished bottle of Valpolicella. We felt a little odd, as if we had unaccountably stepped into someone else's life. But already we also felt a little Venetian, and when we had unpacked I went out to shop. It was almost like coming home.

Seven

Just down the way lay a supermarket, a small place provisioned, like all shops in Venice, by boats from the nearby canal. It was mid-morning now, and the stone-flagged passages of the quarter were crowded with shoppers. Without cars or other transport, Venetians cannot carry too much at one time, so shopping is an almost daily expedition conducted at the helm of little two-wheeled carriers. Even then they take up too much space in narrow aisles so they're left outside – there were a dozen of them standing by the supermarket entrance when I arrived. I found a space and parked my own carrier, a nifty little number patterned in red plaid I'd found behind the apartment door. It was as close as I ever got to a traffic jam in Venice.

Jars of antipasto, mushroom-stuffed ravioli, mozzarella and tomatoes for a salad – I stocked up on whatever lunch-things took my eye. But what interested me as much as the items on the shelves were the customers perusing them. This was not Harry's Bar, the Venice Biennale or a private beach at the Lido, so I wasn't expecting svelte and slinky starlets. But neither was I expecting the quiet diffidence and decorum of these buttoned-up matrons.

You couldn't call Cannaregio's middle-class housewives dowdy. They were well dressed, in a formal, conservative sort of way. Nor were they haughty or standoffish. Here everyone knew everyone else and, when two friends met, long and detailed were their consultative deliberations over the ripeness of the asparagus or the thickness of the Parma ham sliced by the aproned girls behind the meat counter.

But Italy is Italy, and one grows used to its effusiveness, its loud voices and warm, uncalculating spontaneity. That kind of thing was absent here. This wasn't Naples or Rome. Neither was it one of the cooler and more self-possessed north Italian cities

– Turin, say. There seemed to be something else, a distance tinged with some unobtrusive element I couldn't identify that morning. It wasn't something that announced itself with a flourish. But the longer one stays in Venice the more one senses in Venetians a habit of reserve and quiet dignity. It is a quality that seems to have its source in the past.

It is not a character that has anything to do with the city's flamboyant commercial marketing of its history – its carnival or a thousand smaller fêtes and celebrations. You wouldn't find it in a day or two of tramping through noisy museums and across crowd-swept squares. It is something foreigners sense most easily in the atmosphere enveloping the physical city itself, as if it were an element discharged from old brick and undisturbed stone. They are not wrong – such emanations tend to concentrate in obscure places, in still back alleys and along minor canals after dark. But the mood is everywhere, and it was here, too, in the women in the aisles of an ordinary shop on a busy Thursday morning. And it made Venetians seem unlike other Italians.

Was it just a lagoon that separated Venice from the mainland? Or was there a wider distance which made for this quiet sense of a different and largely unconnected past? For a thousand years the Venetian Republic had gazed not to the nearest shore, but eastward, over the lagoon and across the sea. Long ago Venice was the focal point of the Mediterranean, the meeting place of Occident and Orient, an exotic maritime bazaar that became the wealthiest market of commercial exchange in the world. Venetians don't trumpet their past as they once did – their glory is, after all, now well behind them and their foreign ambitions have long fallen away. Today they are simply Italians – and bourgeois, provincial Italians at that. Yet that extravagant Eastern history is always there, no further away than the nearest palace or the faint trace of nostalgia in a Venetian face.

What also remains is a demure regard for the manners of another age. The only uncalculated spontaneity I saw that morning was when a carefully made up shopper, a woman of a certain age, emerged from the supermarket doors with her arms loaded with shopping bags.

'*Ecco la Mamma!*' she trilled effusively to a little white dog tied to a rail beside her carrier. The dog, in return, jumped and wagged its tail, pleased as punch. '*Cara mia! Ecco la Mamma!*' the woman sang again, and if she'd had a tail and no one was watching she might have wagged it, too.

I trundled my own shopping bags back to the apartment, we had lunch, and afterwards Jany stretched out for a siesta. I took myself off outdoors in search a quiet bench in the sun. Less than a hundred yards and just a canal-bridge away from our door lay a large, light-flooded *campo*, one of the squares providing open space in an otherwise cramped and densely-packed city. The Campo dei Gesuiti was silent and deserted when I arrived – in the early afternoon it was inhabited only by a tinkling fountain, by cooing pigeons and sparrows that flitted between trees. Occasionally I had to move benches as the sun slid westward from its zenith, pushing shadows from surrounding buildings across the *campo*'s bright flagstones. But it

123

wasn't enough to disturb my contemplation of what had overnight become our neighbourhood church, the baroque Chiesa dei Gesuiti.

Its façade was vast, an ornate confection of white columns and heavy pediments. Vying for space, an entire community of stone-carved angels, saints and bearded patriarchs cluttered the front of the building. Some were housed in deep, arched niches. Others gave cause for alarm – less cautious, they stood poised on high parapets or teetered precariously from the edge of steep eaves. Of course they ran no risk – from the very top of the church roof, assuring the safety of her heavenly entourage, reigned the Virgin Mary herself.

It was an extraordinary exterior, but nothing compared to the stone-worked wonders that awaited inside. The church's makers seemed to have had a greater love of cloth than stone – they'd contrived to make every surface in the church appear to have been sewn from the softest and most pliant of fabrics. Fat silk pillows, curtains of rippling brocade, an altar covered in bunched swags of damask – all were carved from hard, cold marble. Even the walls themselves appeared to be surfaced in upholstered flock wallpaper. It all made the painting on the first altar to the left, nothing less than an oil by Titian, look meagre and insignificant.

But there was something even more extraordinary about the Gesuiti. Anywhere else such a church would be mobbed, the centrepiece of endless gawking and celebration. But in Venice it was simply a church among a hundred others. For the moment, at least, there were no vast crowds. There were no crowds at all.

The quarter around the Gesuiti slowly came to life after the siesta, and when it did its parishioners hardly seemed to hold the church in special regard. It was mere background to the stuff of daily life. Young mothers in jeans arrived with small children and plonked them down to play on the steps of the church. Dog-walkers stopped to let their dogs lift their legs on its more convenient corners. A pair of girls wobbled around outside it on roller skates. A raucous gang of small boys began slamming a football into its front wall.

'*Goal! Goal!*' they shouted.

'*Va fanculo,*' the goal-keeper, unperturbed and equitable in manner, replied to them all. No one, mothers, babies, dog-walkers, roller-skaters or football-players, gave the Gesuiti a second glance. It was wonderful, this unselfconscious, cheek-by-jowl co-existence of High Baroque and Low Campo. It was all the more wonderful that, apart from me, there wasn't another tourist in sight.

Eventually Jany sauntered by and together we wandered on past the Gesuti to the Fondamenta Nuove. Behind a broad quay land came to a sudden end and the lagoon spread out before us. There were half a dozen *vaporetto* stops along the waterfront. Boats were making off across the water, following staked channel-markers through the lagoon's sand-banks and mud-flats. The islands of San Michele and Murano lay close at hand. Others, further out, sprawled low and indistinct on a flat, hazy horizon.

We carried on past the *vaporetto* halts. There were small restaurants on the quay, where at sunny outdoor tables diners lingered over the detritus of lunch – sauce-stained plates, empty wine bottles and tiny, drained cups of espresso. There were ice cream shops splashing the afternoon with a gaudy touch, a dozen different flavours of *gelati* lined up side by side. Just as colourful was an antique shop dedicated solely to squids – glass squids, brass squids, nimble squids in yellowed lithographs, agile, oil-painted squids in carved and gilded frames. Jany wanted to go inside, but out on the lagoon I was following a different kind of marine traffic.

There were ambulance boats coming our way. They came from various directions every few minutes, some following the shoreline from different parts of the city, others arriving from islands across the lagoon. Like land-bound ambulances they carried red crosses on their sides and blue lights on their roofs. One, an emergency case accompanied by a police boat escort, arrived at high speed in a wash of waves, its lights flashing and siren blaring. The craft were all converging on the same spot, a dock a couple of a hundred yards ahead of us.

'Ospedale Civile', it was sign-posted, and from

freshly arrived boats uniformed nurses and medics were jumping ashore to wheel their patients directly into a quayside hospital complex. I had never seen waterborne health care before. I dragged Jany inside.

The Venice hospital's lagoon-lapped entrance led to even more surprises. The place was vast and ancient, and barely resembled a hospital at all. How could it? It was 600 years old and had seen its beginnings as the Scuola Grande di San Marco, one of the professional associations through which pious Venetians displayed their wealth and benevolence. It had everything a modern hospital could wish for – emergency wards, out-patient clinics, operating theatres, busy staff striding along with stethoscopes around their necks. They all just happened to be housed in the dim, quasi-monastic surroundings of late-medieval Venice.

We wandered about gloomy stone cloisters. We walked down superbly dismal, high-ceilinged hallways. In semi-gloom we passed blue-gowned patients pushing I.V. drip-stands on squeaky wheels. We stumbled across magnificent chapels. We gazed up at ornate ceilings, at religious statuary and age-darkened oil paintings of Christ crucified. I didn't think I'd like to be a patient here. As hospitals go there were too many reminders of the Great Beyond. You got the feeling that in its Christian devotion the place would be more than happy to pack you off into the afterlife at a moment's notice.

But, still, it was pleasing for the same reason that the Gesuiti was pleasing. This was no ordinary institution, yet patients, doctors and visitors all went about their business in an everyday way. Here the sacred blurred into the profane without anyone noticing. The *Ospedale Civile* was humdrum and heavenly at the same time.

It took us twenty minutes to work our way forward to an antique, pillar-lined reception hall. By now we were used to anachronism. It wouldn't have surprised us to stumble out into a street filled with noxious miasmas, masked plague-doctors and tumbrels stuffed with cadavers. But even then I wouldn't have minded. I was beginning to enjoy myself.

Not even confusion on the way back upset my

mood. It is one thing to wander out into the streets of Venice, and quite another to get home again – in the narrow alleys on the far side of the hospital doors we began going around in circles. We squinted at the map. We pored over the guidebook. We took conflicting advice from passers-by. I gave up on conventional navigation and tried Far North survival techniques – I gauged compass direction by the sun, took bearings from prevailing winds. Nothing worked. No visitor, as far as I can make out, has ever explored the streets of Venice without becoming utterly lost.

We wandered for more than an hour, never far from home but never quite there. Finally I realised that maps were useless, grid references a waste of time. In your own neighbourhood you use neighbourhood ways. At the end of a side street I spied a spiffy little shopping carrier pulled by a Venetian matron of a certain age. I had never seen her before but I had little doubt about which supermarket she was headed for.

'*Ecco la mamma! Avanti!*' I said in my best Italian. We followed her, sticking close behind. It took just two right turns, a canal bridge, and a left turn before we were able to drop our pursuit and unlock our front door. It was quite unaccountable: Venice was extraordinary and dramatic, but at the same time ordinary and domestic. Venetian tourism, I decided, was my kind of tourism.

Eight

After our first outing we barely strayed from our own little corner of Cannaregio. If we ventured further it was not towards Saint Mark's Basilica or any other sublime, mobbed monument, but along quiet backwaters and alleys. For the truth was that we had a fairly good idea of the tourist mayhem that lay out there – we just weren't ready to face it.

We wandered minor lanes aimlessly. I began to appreciate small Venetian things – the delicate arch of a bridge reflected in a still canal, the water-eaten stone and crumbling red brick of a once-gorgeous palace, the sudden bright flare of window-boxed geraniums perched high over a dim passageway. The more slowly we went and the less distance we covered, the more of itself Venice revealed.

Jany became even more local than I did. As sociable as ever, she refused to let a small thing like the Italian language hold her back. She used a composite of her own invention, a sort of Esperanto construed on the spot and stitched together from bits of other Latin languages. The astonishing thing was that, helped along by gestures of hands and expressions of face, it actually worked. She used it to chat to Roberto Puppo, the baker from whose next-door *pasticceria* those wonderful drifting odours rose each morning. She used it to gossip to her new friend Monica, a woman so tiny she stood on a raised wooden platform behind the counter of her corner shop. And she used it as she nudged me through the door of every establishment in the neighbourhood.

Together we examined rods and reels laid out on varnished racks in an old-fashioned fishing-tackle shop. In an even more out-dated millinery she guided me through the arcane mysteries of women's foundation garments, hooked, elasticised, flesh-coloured objects so complex in make-up their purpose was unimaginable. In a hotel-trade supplier's we examined chefs' toques, maids' starched caps and yellow-and-black-striped butlers' waistcoats. It wasn't that Jany was actually interested in buying any of these things. She liked them because she liked the people selling them – they were part of the quarter and its solidly-knit neighbourhood life. The shops were old. They were unfashionable. They had personality. And in a fashionable and impersonal place like Venice, a tourist town with an incoming and outgoing population that renewed itself as frequently as the tide, they were a rarity. They were a vaccination against the trials to come.

We couldn't hole up in Cannaregio forever, and a couple of days after our arrival those trials duly arrived, as we knew they must, when we marched in hazy spring sunshine to the *vaporetto* stop by the Rialto Bridge. We might just as easily have gone into the heart of the city on foot. But arriving by water, I enthused to Jany, added a certain Venetian pomp and dignity.

Once the Rialto had been a banking district funding trade between Venice and the East – if you wanted to invest a fortune, exchange currencies, charter a ship, sell a cargo or mount a expedition to the Levant, this was the place to come. But things had changed. We had to fight our way past the tourist-jammed souvenir stalls that now sat at the foot of the humpbacked marble bridge. Where Venetians had once financed an empire they now traded tat.

Mouths agape, we threaded our way through the crowds past Rialto snow-globes and revolting Murano blown glass that looked like glazed vomit. There were pizza plates, Piazza plates, canal calendars and yachtsmen's caps with 'Venezia' scrolled in gold across the brim. And there were gondolas of all sorts – plastic gondolas, key-chain gondolas, blinking plug-in bedside gondolas, battery-operated gondolas that played popular Italian music selections. There were gondolas in bottles, bottles in gondolas, bottles shaped like gondolas.

They were among the more tasteful items. By the time we got to the Italian silk ties printed with anatomically detailed images of female genitalia Jany was snuffling derisively about Venetian pomp and dignity. The greatest days of Venetian commercial glory, I had to admit, seemed to have come and gone. But I wasn't worried. Just a short boat-ride away lay Saint Mark's Basilica and the Ducal Palace. Hadn't Ruskin himself called the palace 'the central building of the world'? If Venice was making money flogging pornographic neckties to all the peoples of the earth it also did a profitable line in art and high culture.

Fifteen minutes later we jumped off a *vaporetto* onto the most frantic stretch of waterfront in all Venice. In front of us lay Saint Mark's Basin, that broad expanse of water which funnels traffic into the mouth of the Grand Canal. But it was not nearly as busy as the Riva degli Schiavoni, the quay that lines it. Joining the crowd on the Riva was like falling into a fast-flowing current. One moment Jany and I were standing on its edge, marvelling at the force of its surge; the next we were swept helplessly along on a human tide. There was no end to the restless, roiling mix of races and languages and nationalities. Away it tumbled in a fluid, continuous spate, the upheld flags and umbrellas of tour-group leaders showing the speed of the crowd's advance.

It was no good trying to make for calm backwaters. Once we got snagged at the end of a stand selling carnival masks and bell-tinkling court jester's hats. Once we swirled about in an eddy of hotel guests struggling to the front door of the Danieli. Once we were caught in a log-jam of photographers snapping pictures of the Bridge of Sighs. It was only a couple of hundred yards further on that the torrent slowed and finally came to a halt in the great arcaded space of the Piazza San Marco. Like victims of shipwreck washed ashore, we were at last deposited in front of the Ducal Palace in the heart of Venice.

I had no complaints about a Japanese tour-group, the large party that preceded us up the Scala d'Oro and on through the Palace – they were as inconspicuous and self-effacing as any couple of hundred people can be. But I can still hear their buzz of excitement, see the massed video cameras swing back and forth in unison as a Japanese guide's commentary unreeled at high speed. In the world of art and

138

culture the Palazzo Ducale has become a supreme example of European architectural refinement. In my own memory, though, its great halls will remain forevermore a venue for the holding of large oriental sporting events.

Around we went. The palace was huge, the pace relentless. Not speaking Japanese, the details of the building's transition from Gothic to Renaissance remained a mystery to me. But I think it would be fair to say that both periods relied heavily on lavish displays of gilt. There were huge swatches of it everywhere. Burnished and gleaming, it encrusted walls, dripped from cornices, and ran in crested waves across ceilings. Much of it surrounded even huger swatches of oil painting.

Still feeling fresh and curious, we walked around the Sala dello Scudo, the Shield Room, a hall in which the Doges received foreign visitors they wished to impress. In other rooms we had seen works by Venetians whose names are known by millions – Tintoretto, Tiepolo, Veronese. In the Shield Room I looked at works by artists I'd never heard of before.

I'm not sure that Ramusio, Gastaldi or Zorzi were household names for other people, either.

Why, then, had their artistry so impressed the Doge's foreign visitors? It hadn't – it was the theme they'd depicted. Spread across the Sala della Scudo's high walls were painted maps, representations of the Venetian Republic's once vast and scattered maritime trading empire.

I looked up at oil-painted charts of the Dalmatian littoral, of Cyprus, Crete, the Peloponnese, the scattered islands off Asia Minor, the wide coast sweeping around the eastern end of the Mediterranean. Everywhere there – by negotiation, by purchase, by stealth and sometimes by outright aggression – Venice had acquired the imperial possessions she used to promote trade with the East.

I strained to read the script on the maps. Zara, Zakinthos, Monemvasia, Negroponte, the Morea ... they were hardly place-names that reverberate in the annals of global trade today. But even at the height of her power most of Venice's territories were small and isolated coastal sites – islands, seaside cities, ports, sometimes nothing more than fortresses on rocky and defended headlands. Yet with them Venice established an imperial network, multiple strings of possessions rarely more than a day's sailing apart, joining the head of the Adriatic to the great trading terminals of the Levant.

For 500 years they had made her the richest and most powerful maritime nation in the eastern Mediterranean. It was the empire shown on these walls that was the source of the city's great wealth, that spawned her power, prestige and displays of opulence. It was the empire's trading prosperity that had allowed painters like Tintoretto and Veronese to exist in the first place. If Venice had produced the most sophisticated art of its age, it was sophisticated trade that had produced Venice.

Jany had moved on down vast, wide hallways. Alone, I continued gazing up at far-flung islands and thinking of how they had become Venetian. This was one of those moments, inevitable in a place where you could hardly sidestep the Mediterranean's rich and complex past, where I was going to have to confront a large chunk of history head-on. It was daunting – the island in the lagoon might have been called *la Serenissima*, the Most Serene Republic, but her centuries were long and crowded and anything but serene.

Venice, I knew, had never been interested in acquiring the territorial holdings of a true overseas empire. While she had possessions on the Italian mainland, her ventures there had more often than not got her into big trouble with powerful neighbours. Her good luck lay precisely in *not* being on the mainland. The lagoon gave her protection, and in her isolation placed her strategically between West and East. Her opportunity came in linking the two – she made it her business to connect the wealth of Europe with the valuable and hard-to-obtain resources of Asia. And so her aims were not ownership of land on either continent, but control of the sea that lay between them.

One result of this was that Venice had little use for the kind of moral rationale required by other huge empires. Unlike Alexander the Great before her, she felt no need to impose political unity on the world by force of arms. Unlike the British after her, she claimed no improving mission, no need to export a superior way of life to lesser peoples. Unlike the Spanish in the New World, she was inspired by no zeal, driven by no religious ideal to convert the heathen – Venice, in fact, was often cursed by other Christian powers for her willingness to do business with Muslims even in times of holy war. In Venice, profit drove all before it.

But every nation, even those unashamedly bent on commercial gain, needs ideological unity, some sort of cohesive, underlying spirit that justifies and propels its venture forward. Where, I had to ask, was Venice's? Then I walked a few short feet into the next room of the Ducal Palace. Here was my answer. The Sala Grimani was a lair containing half a dozen winged, stone-carved lions.

They served merely as reminders, for lions, of course, are everywhere in Venice. One sentence alone – a rather long one at that – ensures that readers of Jan Morris's superb study *Venice* are given ample feeling for the leonine presence in the city: 'The city crawls with lions, winged lions and ordinary lions, great lions and petty lions, lions on doorways, lions supporting windows, lions on corbels, self-satisfied lions in gardens, lions rampant, lions soporific, amiable lions, ferocious lions, soporific lions, vivacious lions, dead lions, rotting lions, lions on chimneys, on flowerpots, on garden gates, on crests, on medallions, lurking among foliage, blatant on pillars, lions on flags, lions on tombs, lions in pictures, lions at the feet of statues, lions realistic, lions symbolic, lions heraldic, lions archaic, mutilated lions, chimerical lions, semi-lions, super-lions, lions with elongated tails, feathered lions, lions with jewelled eyes, marble lions, porphyry lions, and one real lion, drawn from the life, as the artist proudly says, by the indefatigable Longhi, and hung among the rest of his genre pictures in the Querini-Stampalia gallery.'

That, surely, is a sufficiency of lions; I won't bother readers with the slightest account of the six specimens I bumped into the Doge's Palace. But Morris's description only further begged the question, and I lingered on in front of them. Venice was lion-obsessed. What was this heraldic icon so deeply buried in the city's psyche? Obviously it could be nothing less than essential to Venice's existence, a symbol of the energy that drove her.

Of all Venice's lions its most famous is the three-ton bronze beast who lives atop a granite pillar on the waterside Molo just outside the Doge's Palace. Probably the most didactic lion as well, its placing in this prominent public place reminded Venetians of their city's origins.

For the winged lion is, of course, the apostolic symbol of Saint Mark. And even if the saint's association with Venice is largely based on myth, it was as necessary to the greatness of this port-city as Alexander's legend was to Alexandria. Only with Saint Mark's posthumous elevation to the post of supreme patron of the Republic did the city itself climb to its dizziest heights.

Early Venice, by contrast, couldn't have started from a lower point. When the western half of the Roman Empire collapsed in the barbarian invasions of the 5th century Venice did not collapse with it

– barely exposed mud-banks have nowhere to go but up. Of no interest at all until then, the uninhabited islands of the lagoon became a refuge, a haven for mainlanders escaping waves of attacks by murderous barbarians. Safely isolated, Venice gradually grew into permanent island-communities built on wooden piles driven into the muck. And with them also grew the self-reliance of a people with no other resource to exploit than the liquid expanse that surrounded them. From the start Venetians were as happy afloat as ashore, as amphibious in their lagoon as swamp-frogs in a pond.

If the first Venetians made a living trading across the lagoon, they had to search further for their religious needs. And there was only one direction to look in – eastwards. With the West overrun and Rome in pagan hands the capital of Christianity was transferred to the eastern half of the empire. It was from Constantinople, the new Roman capital established in AD 324 in the old Greek city of Byzantium, that the power of the church radiated. Patriarchs and governors dispatched from Constantinople dispensed not just holy communion in Venice, but political instruction, too. Byzantine by administration, Venice became partly Eastern, also, in her taste and outlook, her love of refinement and sensual display. It was one reason why Venice was so at ease in her later trade in the East – she felt pretty well at home there already.

Venice may have begun as an oriental city, but as she grew so did the contest with authority in faraway Constantinople. Venetians, always independent spirits, elected their first Doge in the early 700s. It was a move towards self-rule which under 117 successive Doges was to develop into a kind of government found nowhere else. And it was rule with staying power – more than a thousand years were to pass before the *Serenissima*'s republican independence was finally extinguished by Napoleon.

I watched a teenage brother and sister slouch into the Sala Grimani behind their parents. They were bored stupid, and suddenly, in front of the lions, they declared they'd had enough. In this day and age, of course, bucking parental authority is expected – despite protests they simply told their father they

147

wanted money for pizza. He gave it to them and they stomped off.

For young dependencies in the medieval age telling parent-states to go and get lost wasn't quite as simple. A century after Venice's first elections, a line of Popes was re-ensconced in Rome and dual Christian empires, Eastern and Western, had agreed to separate spheres of influence. The city on the water, squeezed between the two, wanted neither of them. Determined on a separate existence, she looked about for some way of signalling her intentions.

What Venice needed was a symbol, a talisman whose divine power would protect her identity and autonomy. In fact she already had a patron, the saint who today still bravely shares the top of a second granite pillar on the Molo with a crocodile. But Theodore was ignored – he was a symbol of Byzantine origin. Had that other evangelical power, Saint Peter, been available, he might have been enlisted instead. But he was already employed by the Holy See in Rome. With both protectors in the service of other states, the Venetians, never ones to let religious principle stand in the way of practical need, came up with their own source of domestic help. They engaged Saint Mark, concocting for him a CV that was doubtful from the very beginning.

Mark, so the Venetian creation-myth goes, set off one day for Rome from Aquileia, a city lying on the Adriatic to the east of Venice. Why he would choose to navigate the dangerous and deserted channels of the lagoon is not explained, but during the crossing a great storm arose and Mark's boat, propelled by a divine wind, was pushed onto a mudbank. An angel sent from God then appeared before the saint and intoned, '*Pax tibi, Marce, Evangelista Meus. Hic requiscet corpus tuum*' – 'Peace be unto you, Mark, my evangelist. In this place your body shall rest'. What the angel went on to say, the legend insists, was that Christians would one day settle the swamps and build a magnificent city as a repository of Mark's body.

Such a prophecy, put about many centuries after Mark's supposed marooning, was all very well and good. But a body was needed – this was still an age in which the physical remains of early Church leaders bestowed a potent aura upon any city that possessed them. And so a body was found. In 828 two Venetian merchants removed the remains of Mark from his tomb in Alexandria, the city where he'd been bishop for the last forty years of his life. His shroud, so the accounts go, was cut open and the body of another saint, which by good fortune happened to be lying nearby, was stuffed into its place. The deception failed – so aromatically scented with heavenly purity was the odour exuding from Mark's 800-year-old corpse that the theft was noticed and the alarm immediately raised. When the Venetians hauled the body aboard their ship only the ruse of hiding it in a consignment of pork saved it from discovery by suspicious Muslim harbour officials.

So did Venice, celebrity body snatcher, come into possession of a relic that gave it a spiritual mystique just slightly less prestigious than Rome's. (Only in 1968, in a commemoration nineteen centuries after Mark's martyrdom, did the Catholic Church consent to return the relic – and then merely a portion of it – to Alexandria.) Once she had the saint, Venice set about building her distinctive character around him. A gorgeous reliquary was built to house Mark's remains – it would later become Venice's great Basilica. '*Pax tibi, Marce, Evangelista Meus*', the words that appeared on the book held in the paw of Venetian lions, became a slogan of Venetian identity. For centuries Saint Mark's banner sailed ahead of Venetian fleets of massed war galleys. It flew before Venetian armies who trumpeted '*Viva San Marco!*' as they stormed into battle. From Spalato to Famagusta and throughout the Venetian domains the saint's standard fluttered over ports and palaces, churches, fortresses and governor's residences.

Not even a great fire that destroyed the early basilica and obliterated Mark's remains in the 11th century could hold the city's patron back. Mark's body had not been consumed in the flames, it turned out. It had simply been misplaced. For in the middle of a commemoration service held by the Doge after the basilica's rebuilding a miracle took place. There was a cracking sound from a church column, a sudden fissuring of stone, and lo! Saint Mark's hand abruptly emerged into the daylight, to be duly followed by his entire and wondrously-preserved body. It was hardly a surprise – with a sponsor of this resilience at the helm, Venice could only move from strength to glorious strength. Saint Mark, a direct witness of the word of God and incombustible to boot, could guarantee nothing less.

Suddenly Jany was pulling at my shirtsleeve. She barely glanced at the weathered, stone-cut lions I was still standing by.

'Are you asleep? she said. 'You haven't moved an inch in the last ten minutes. I've been through outer waiting rooms and inner waiting rooms, the Sala del Collegio, the chamber of the Senate and the Scala dei Censori. And there's still a lot more. Aren't you coming? It's exhausting.'

So off we moved, this time on the heels of a frantically noisy Italian tour group. Our ears ringing, our eyes slowly glazing over, we trudged through one thronged and gilded room after another. The larger the hall, the more spectacular the paintings became. By the time we got to the Sala del Maggior Consiglio

– a meeting-room so massive it could accommodate the 2,500 members of Venice's Great Council – we had ceased to take in anything at all. The further we went the less we cared. We were tired, thirsty, overheated and becoming claustrophobic. The last bits of the palace went by in a forgettable blur, and finally we were out on the Piazza San Marco again.

I stood on the edge of the jammed square, thinking not just of the acres of gilded halls that lay behind us, but of the myth that went with them. Is there any point in trying to separate the historical from the fictional in a city built on the legend of a Christian saint? It would be like trying to demystify Che Guevara or the cowboys of the American West – historical reality, in the end, is driven by such fictions. What is certain is that in Saint Mark Venice found a figure around which a new kind of pride could coalesce – nationalism.

It was a more focussed kind of pride than that which had caused the two ice cream-licking backpackers in front of me to sew Canadian flags on their rucksacks. Of all the Italian city-states, Venice was the only one to escape centuries of feudal autocracy. Over time she moved from a rough kind of egalitarian democracy to an unyielding patrician rule that muzzled popular expression. But throughout, the city remained a mercantile city. In other societies across Europe the development of a commercial class was held back by its conflict with an aristocracy. In Venice a commercial class *was* the aristocracy, and its values pervaded the whole society.

The religious fervour that surrounded Saint Mark transformed itself into tremendous civic self-esteem and an identification with the Republic and its institutions. Allegiance that elsewhere might have gone to the nobility or the church was in Venice attached directly to the state. 'They want to appear as Christian before the world,' Pope Pius II complained from Rome, 'but in reality they never think of God and, but for the state, which they regard as a deity, they hold nothing sacred.'

Unity, in its turn, led to single-minded energy in Venice's pursuit of profit. If the *Serenissima*'s overseas adventures were primarily undertaken for the benefit of her wealthy merchant-princes, they were also seen to contribute to the greater glory of the city and all its inhabitants. And in art, in architecture and music, in the prestige and prosperity of the population as a whole, they did. Venice became the envy of the world. It was this fierce proto-nationalism, combined with unrivalled ability in all matters commercial and sea-faring, which kept Venice far ahead of her competitors – for a time, at any rate.

A good deal of that commercial skill had remained – square yard for square yard, I was willing to bet there were more tourists packed onto this piazza paying higher prices for ice cream than anywhere else on the continent.

But success has its price – nowhere else on the continent is mass tourism so at odds with its surroundings. Behind the Canadian backpackers an overweight child fed pigeons while his overweight father took photos. Sandals removed for a picnic, toes pale in the grime that rimmed them, a woman sat on the Piazza steps beside us spreading cream cheese on crackers. Around us milled tour parties, families

and school-groups from every part of the planet —
hip-hop boys in baggy clothes and baseball caps;
punks with barbed-wire tattoos around their biceps
and beer cans in their hands; parties of silver-haired,
name-tagged retirees; files of small children winding
their way across the Piazza. Off in the distance tourist
queues snaked away from the doors of the Basilica and
Campanile only to disappear around far corners.

Closer by, a band in dinner jackets was stationed
outside the Caffè Quadri and racing through a frenzied
medley of Eastern European gypsy music — the end
of each refrain concluded with the violinists, madly
sawing away, flinging up their bows and shouting
'Hey!' Jany wandered over to the Caffè Florian to see
if it looked any more restful, but wandered back to
report it was crowded with tourists taking photos of
other tourists drinking €14.00 aperitifs.

We were all the same. We had come to be amazed
and entertained by Venice. In her Mediterranean conviviality Jany was as sociable as anyone on the entire
square. But this kind of sociability was beyond her.

'Did you know,' I observed, 'that your compatriot

Napoleon called the Piazza the finest drawing room of Europe?'

'Yes, I did,' Jany replied. 'But I doubt he ever imagined the whole continent trying to barge its way in at the same time. Let's go home. This is awful.'

I had to agree. Just at the moment our own little drawing room looked even finer. So dragging sore feet, we headed for home and a bath. We'd had enough art and culture for one day.

Nine

Why does tourism make us all so stupid? It was something I had to ask myself as, day in and day out for the next week, we were swept with countless thousands around the marbled magnificence of Venice.

Dutifully, we ascended the three floors of the sprawling Correr Museum, there inspecting Venetian coin collections, ducal regalia, hideous ceramics and Carpaccio's arresting 'Young man in a Red Hat'. We marched solemnly through the church of Santi Giovanni e Paolo, gawking at the family tombs of the Mocenigo Doges, the foot of Saint Catherine of Siena, and an urn containing the flayed skin of Marcantonio Bragadin, the Venetian commander peeled alive by his captor Lala Mustafa Pasha at the Turkish siege of Famagusta in 1571. Battling through crowds, we discovered furniture suites of green and gold lacquer in the Ca' Rezzonico, canal views by Canaletto, and a beast by Longhi – not a lion drawn, as the artist proudly says, from the life, but his equally animated 'Rhinoceros'. Few creations of any kind escaped our attentions.

And yet the more I saw the more I wondered about the impetus that drove us relentlessly around Venice like voracious army ants.

When we leave our homes for holidays in places like Venice we set out as functioning human beings. We're more or less in control of our lives. We have jobs that demand capable performance, relationships that need subtle handling, household tasks that require regular attention. We manage in a complex world. If we are not able to fix a car ourselves we know where there's a Midas Muffler that can.

Then we arrive at our destination and suddenly there is barely an area in which we have any competence left at all. We don't know the difference between a Tintoretto and a Veronese. We stumble through restaurant menus even when they're in four languages, one of them our own. We can't get around the corner, much less from the Palazzo Gritti to the Galleria Franchetti, without getting hopelessly lost. We might as well be mentally impaired three-year-olds.

In the normal course of travel these things aren't a problem – they are what make travel interesting and worthwhile in the first place. You learn that you prefer Bellini to either Tintoretto or Veronese, you discover that *figadini* delights your tastebuds and *fegato* doesn't. Eventually you even find your way from the palace to the gallery. You make the world a bigger place. But as time went by I began to wonder if the world was really becoming bigger at all – more often it seemed the same confusing place with just a lot more people in it. Venetian tourism was starting to bother me in a serious way.

Was I becoming a travel snob? Or were these vast tour parties, herded by their group-leaders through one gallery and palace after another, really as sheep-like as they looked? In the circumstances it was difficult to be anything else. It was the scale of the operations that made it all so doubtful. Venice, a vast concentration of art, was also a vast exploitation of art.

'It's like the Vegas Venice, only much, much better,' a woman marvelled to us one day as, standing in a *vaporetto*, we steamed past Gothic arches and flamboyant tracery on the Grand Canal. Who cares what Venice really is, or was? Today's kind of tourism doesn't offer a lot of scope to find out. It is a hungry maw down which ordinarily competent people disappear to be transformed into dim-witted gawkers. The really odd thing is that they welcome such transformation and go to it willingly.

For me it all came to a head on the afternoon we finally decided to visit the Basilica. Day after day we had been putting it off because the lines stretching away beneath its domes and golden kiosks had been so long. It was the one place that not only I, but everyone else in Venice, especially wanted to see.

And with reason. Inside and out, it is the most extraordinary sight in the city. No one could take it for a simple church. It is too gaudy, too wild and extravagant to be a place of worship. The poet Petrarch thought it the most beautiful thing on earth. Mark Twain enjoyed it for its 'entrancing, tranquilizing, soul-satisfying ugliness'. Ruskin thought it 'a treasure-heap ... a confusion of delight'. Herman Melville saw it as charmingly impermanent, as if 'the Grand Turk had pitched his pavilion here for a summer day'. Not even Twain, though, a man who devoted an entire book to the still new and baffling spectacle of tourism, had any idea how big the monster he was describing would eventually become.

And it remains more baffling than ever. Why would people wait an hour, even two hours or more, I wondered, only to rush through the Basilica in less than ten minutes?

For here was the building, a sort of sacred trophy-house, that lodged the city's soul. Much of its treasure was plunder, pure and simple. No matter – such booty honoured God, Venice and the ideal of material gain equally, and for centuries a dazzling exhibition had encouraged congregations to ever greater efforts. Here were worked porphyry blocks filched from Acre; sculpted columns stolen in Syria; the stone-carved Tetrarchs taken from Roman Alexandria; the Horses of San Marco, looted from Constantinople. And that was just on the outside of the building. Inside, pickings from the same Byzantine adventure were everywhere. Nor did the Venetians feel any need to dissemble their ill-gotten wealth as art. The vast majority of gold and silver objects ransacked from Constantinople lay in the Treasury, a glittering horde of reliquaries, chalices, incense burners, icons and candelabra. Having heard of these things, I was anxious to see them all.

But I didn't. The visit didn't go well from the beginning. We queued for forty minutes. I was told I would not be allowed inside with the shoulder bag I was carrying. I returned breathless from the apartment to find Jany already gone in. I waited another hour to get to the front of the queue again. Out of nowhere a brazen German stepped into the line in front of me. I objected. He said my objections were useless. I said if he went ahead of me he would be breaking the rules of acceptable conduct. He said if I went ahead of him he would be breaking my face. So did matters proceed until I finally entered the Basilica.

Inside the doors stood movable metal railings, the kind used at terrorist bomb scenes, Jamaican carnivals, British cup-final victory parades and other lunatic gatherings. Here parallel lines of railing formed a corridor, about six feet wide, running up one side of the church and down the other. It was jammed with bodies and we shuffled along, looking left and right as we proceeded.

I suppose there were arterial corridors leading off to the Treasury and up to the Horses on the roof. I didn't see them. I was so dismayed by the whole pack'em-in-'n-move'em-along atmosphere that I didn't see much of anything at all. Even the Basilica's floor-mosaics, a display of colours and patterns almost as astonishing as the wall mosaics too distant to see properly, were invisible beneath our feet – they were covered by a protective layer, a sort of springy grey Astroturf. Moving at the same speed as everyone else,

I was through the church and out into bright daylight once more almost before I knew it.

Venice's thousand years had passed before my eyes in just over nine minutes. I couldn't be bothered to queue up to repeat the process, and never saw the wonders of the Basilica again. The place left me speechless.

Ten

Mid-morning had passed and still we lay in bed, listening to the upstairs neighbour's piano and wondering how to spend the day. We were burned out, wholly fed up with churches and museums. Then, stepping out to buy *pan di Domenica*, the special bread Puppo's Pasticceria sold only on Sundays, Jany had an idea. For the residents of Cannaregio Sunday seemed to be made for excursions and family visits – dapperly dressed and fresh from Mass, customers emerged from Puppo's with bunches of spring flowers in one hand and boxed cakes tied with ribbons in the other.

Why didn't we make an outing of it too, Jany suggested, and get away from Venice altogether? Not far away lay the islands of the lagoon. The idea of not seeing another alabaster-cheeked cherub or

Madonna and Child for an entire day cheered us tremendously.

Down on the Fondamenta Nuove the sun was shining in a limpid sky. Waiting on the quay with other island excursionists, we gazed out across the lagoon. For all its brightness the Venetian day was restrained – soft and pearly-hued and a little blurred. The atmosphere played games with distance and perspective. The horizon seemed to sit too high and it was difficult to say how far across the water church or campanile lay. I reminded myself, as I often had to, that this was still part of the Mediterranean. Not far away from our own home the Marseilles sun, like the working-class city it rose upon, was plain and unambiguous. There the light was strong, contours were clear and objects simply defined. And so it was elsewhere in this sea. But nothing is quite as simple in Venice. It has no hesitation in informing you, through a thousand variations of light and colour, that it is a more subtle place. It stands apart from its sister cities and, despite common origins, denies kinship with any of them.

Soon our *vaporetto* slid into the landing. Passengers piled on and piled off, and with a sudden thrust of propellers and a back-surge of water we were away. It seemed as easy as boarding a city bus, but just how the passenger ferries coped was a mystery to me. I watched our skipper throw his engine into reverse and nonchalantly flip the spokes of his wheel to turn his boat's stern, allowing an incoming *vaporetto* all of six inches' clearance. Could anything but maritime genes a hundred generations old allow such calculation?

Jany and I passed on through the main cabin of the *vaporetto*, a place of crowded wooden benches and loud chatter. Through glass doors we spotted two unoccupied seats on the boat's tiny, open rear deck. There was a sharp, fresh tang in the air that never seemed to reach the confines of narrow Venetian streets. Gulls hovered so close we could see their greedy eyes casting about for passengers to toss them food. As the vaporetto rounded San Michele we sat filling our lungs and looking behind to the broad, milky-green arc of our wake. It didn't matter that we were sailing on a shallow lagoon and surrounded by hidden mudbanks. We had escaped – after the closeness of Venice we felt we'd cast off on a wide and liberating sea.

Murano was far too busy to disembark. So were Torcello and Burano. But at Mazzorbo nobody got off, so we did. The little island was quiet and peaceful. On a day of Sunday visits, the busiest people about were the living paying their respects to the dead in the island's green and leafy cemetery.

We walked beside the sun-flooded lagoon and I felt more relaxed than I had in weeks. Water has that effect. So, too, does lunch eaten outdoors in spring sunshine. When we came to the little waterside Trattoria della Madalena and saw tables overlooking a quiet channel we sat down without even consulting each other. I had the sole. Jany had the *frutta di mare mista*. She looked happier than Tintoretto's 'Virgin Ascending to Heaven'. It wasn't just the food. It was the sweetness of the day and the softness of the lagoon air that made for our humour. That, and perhaps the steadily descending bottle of wine.

By the time we were finished the world had

become the mellow kind of place where all things are reconciled. We sat basking in the sun watching boats come up the channel. A few were tour vessels – packed, double-decked craft with loudspeakers mounted in the bow. More were local, families in small day-cruisers or young men impressing girls in speedboats. But the happiest-looking Venetians to go by were three crewmen on a *topo*, one of those tireless delivery boats found in every canal in the city.

Taking the day off, they lay splayed on the foredeck, their torsos bare, their tanned faces giving way to dead white in a sudden V at their necks. They may have been the hardest-working people in the city, but at the moment they had about them the satisfied appearance of men who owned all they surveyed.

I couldn't help thinking that once, long ago, it had been more than just appearance. But history's wheels had turned and Venice's maritime prerogative was lost. There wasn't much left but floating delivery jobs. It seemed a tiny inheritance from an extraordinary past. Did nothing else remain?

In one sense it did. Venice had in fact lost none of

the business flair that had generated such prosperity for so long. The city had adapted to circumstances. Having created history through its wealth, it had turned around and learned to create wealth through its history. Instead of going out to the world for money, it was clever enough to persuade the world to bring it to Venice. And no matter how quickly the city slimmed down the fattest wallets, it did so with manners and style. The tourists, despite great crowds of other tourists, kept on coming.

But it seemed to me that there was something deeper that Venice had lost for good – its cosmopolitan character.

It didn't matter how worldly the guests at the Gritti Palace were. It didn't matter which languages were spoken on the Piazza or how many races and nationalities blended on the Riva degli Schiavoni. Real cosmopolitanism comes from exchange based on mutual interest. Mass tourism might have its own exchanges, its payments for services rendered, but the relationship is one-sided and temporary. Today tourists arrive at destinations all over the world, pay for what they want – sunshine or sex or art – and then leave. Of genuine shared benefits in the largest industry on the globe there are few.

Sitting on the edge of Mazzorbo and watching those *topo* men pass by, it came to me I wanted another kind of Venice. And I knew, too, that I was looking straight at it – a more watery Venice. Painting and architecture might be the elegant froth that floated on the city's surface, but beneath it lay the lagoon and the sea, long the basis of Venetian existence. I'd had enough tourism for a while.

I spent the rest of the day quietly plotting a mutiny, and the next morning, bright and early, presented myself at the Palazzo Loredan, Venice's town hall.

Escorted upstairs, I was shown into the office of Caterina Faloma. It was a small, busy place, full of stacks of paper and people shouting '*Pronto*!' into telephones. Signorina Faloma, blonde and energetic, had plenty on her hands. But when I explained what I was interested in, she showed all the vigour and organisational talent the Venetians are renowned for.

'The sea?' she mused. 'You want to know how Venetians live with the sea? Yes, it is a big question. How could we not live with the sea? You must give me a minute.'

It hardly took longer than that. Soon she was on the telephone, and before lunchtime had presented me with names, dates and telephone numbers – a whole sheaf of suggestions.

'First, you must see the Arsenale, this very afternoon. It was the world's first shipyard, the place where they built Venetian galleys. I have spoken to Comandante Calzavara – he is arranging it. And you should visit the Archivio di Stato. It is wonderful, an old monastery full of monks' cells – it holds every Venetian document ever written about land or sea. The Dotoressa Alessandra Schiavon is the archival director, and she will help you.

'Do you like sailing? There is a yacht, a famous racing boat called the *Moro de Venezia*: next weekend it will escort a regatta through the lagoon. You will meet Corrado Scrascia, a Venetian sailor. And rowing, you like rowing? A few days later there is a race for

caorlinas, the market boats that used to deliver vegetables to Venice. They are very heavy, and need seven
rowers. You can follow the race with Umberto Sichiro
– nobody knows more about rowing. You are interested in gondolas, too? There is only one man to see
– Gianfranco Vianello. He is a champion rower, and
one of the best gondola-builders in Venice.'

I was thrilled – here was a watery Venice I had
only glimpsed from a distance. I could hardly ask for
more. But then I did. And before she sat down to
her antipasti Caterina Faloma put a call through to
yet another Venetian waterman, Renato Barich, of
Barich Trasporti. I was enlisted, if only temporarily,
as a canal delivery man. *Topo* toil wasn't easy, I was
warned – the work was hard and the hours long. But
walking back to my own lunch I felt happy. I might
have been a *sandolo*, the lightest and most dapper of
Venetian craft, floating exuberantly on a rising lagoon
tide.

Eleven

Overheard in the Museo Storico Navale, the historical naval museum that sits outside the walls of the Venice Arsenal:

English father to teenage son – Here's an old British Army joke. How many gears does an Italian tank have?

Son – I don't know. One?

Father – No, four. One forward and three in reverse. Ha, ha!

It wasn't the world's funniest joke, but if it had to be told I could see why it was being told here. Venice's vast naval museum was partly devoted to recent history, including the last World War's – the rooms I was strolling through held underwater mines, models of camouflage-grey destroyers and the bells of famous ships. But there were also a number of Italian 'secret weapons' of 1940s vintage. In technological terms they might have appeared devilishly cunning at the time, but they didn't look that way now. They looked like the kind of fiendish device that Q might have designed for James Bond if Q had just had a lobotomy.

The apparatus that father and son were standing in front of was a tiny metal vessel with a powerful motor, an open cockpit and just one seat. Labelled 'Explosive Speedboat' in English and Italian, such craft, the accompanying notice explained, had been employed in the Second World War in action at Suda Bay. It carried a powerful charge designed to detonate on contact with a target, and its use was simple: 'at about 200 metres the pilot blocked the rudder and jettisoned using the floating seat-back.' A floating seat-back! Those Italian naval engineers had certainly thought of everything. Still, I had my doubts. Why was the explosive speedboat used on only one occasion?

There was more zany-scientist stuff. There was a

'Waterproof Container for Carrying Assault Craft' – a sort of outsize cigar tube holding a cylindrical attack-boat designed to be 'attached to a submarine deck and used in a concealed approach to the entrance of enemy bases'. Was the assault craft waterproof, too, and launched from a submerged submarine? How were the expelled attackers – wet or dry – to get back into their submarine? It wasn't explained. But clearly the Italians had been conducting daring and innovative underwater experiments. There was also a mannequin dressed in an Italian frogman's prototype wetsuit. He had his oxygen tanks on his chest and wore aqua-dynamic rubber shoes so tapered and foppishly pointy that a 14th-century courtier would have loved them. It all seemed a little medieval.

But then I walked a little further and suddenly Venice's naval museum *was* medieval. And the older it got the more impressive it became. How can you not be impressed by a 400-year-old tiller more than nine feet long and adorned with a dragon's head? A tiller, what's more, that belonged to an oar-driven war-galley, a ship whose design was already old when it was adopted by the Greeks and Romans? So confident were the Venetians in the efficiency of their formidable galleys that they used them well into the 17th century. Looking at that tiller, a small remnant of what was in effect the Venetian marine version of a tank, I could practically guarantee it – no opponent seeing one of Venice's earlier triremes bearing down on him, its three tiers of flashing oars powered by 250 men, would have found time for making jokes. Venetian galleys didn't go in reverse and their top gear – ramming speed – wasn't funny at all.

And so I continued walking on around the museum, cutting my time as fine as I dared – I didn't want to miss my meeting with Comandante Calzavara and his assistant, Patrizia Rigo, at the gates of the Arsenale. But who could resist the carved wooden stern-ornament from Admiral Morosini's 17th-century flagship, a top-knotted Turk bound in chains? Or a 300-year-old glass ship's lantern, surmounted by a fretted-metal lion of Saint Mark, the size of a Volkswagen van?

There were models of galleons and galliots, fustas

and frigates, barques, brigantinos, and a dozen other kinds of Venetian craft. And they, too, surprised me – most of them were propelled by oars. The Venetians, having started life in a shallow, difficult-to-navigate lagoon, were always more comfortable with manpower than sails – they still prefer to row today. What astonished me were the distances they rowed back then.

From the beginning Venetians had rowed their warships. But from the 1300s they began to row their cargo-ships, too. It didn't sound like a brilliant move – it sounded like a step backwards. But it came down to a question of speed. With the growth of their markets in the East, with the rise of competitors like Genoa in the West, with the dangers of piracy along the way, the Venetians had to be fast. And, quite simply, given the technology of the day, they could row faster than they could sail. Perhaps they also had more incentive than most galley-rowers – the men weren't slaves, but free and well paid. Nor were they ever more than a day's row from rest in a Venetian port. When the winds were right they even got a little help by hoisting sails. Nonetheless, just imagining it gave me lumbar spasms. Men who could row from Venice all the way up to the Black Sea, load freight and then row back again were not men to be ignored.

Nor was their successor, Comandante Calzavara. What very nearly made me late for my rendezvous was a detailed scale model of a boat that had never been rowed very far at all. The state ship, the *Bucintoro*, rarely made it past the mouth of the lagoon. And maybe that was a good thing – it was built more for ceremony than seaworthiness. Not even Cleopatra's royal Nile barge had been quite as extravagant.

I gazed on. The *Bucintoro* had been 140 feet long and powered below decks by 168 men, four to an oar. Above decks the Doge, pre-eminent among Venetians at sea as on land, had presided from his high throne at the head of a spacious salon. State dignitaries sat in attendance below him. No matter how grandiose their behaviour, how rich their robes, not even they could add a great deal more to the lavishness of the display. Festooned with heavy gilt, ivory, satins, embroidered damasks and other precious materials, the *Bucintoro* was a voluptuous symbol honouring the *Serenissima*'s eternal ties to the sea. From the winged lion on her bowsprit to the proliferation of carved sphinxes, mermaids, dragons and sea monsters disporting themselves across her hull, she was a declaration of the glory of maritime Venice.

Ten minutes later I was at the gates of the Arsenale, a decorative entrance set in two miles of high and forbidding walls. The gates continued to hint at maritime fantasy – carved, trident-wielding sea gods still guarded the way in. But on the other side of the wall all self-indulgence stopped. The Arsenale remains an active naval base and out of bounds to civilians – once through a check-point I was surrounded by the kind of spit, polish and purposeful bustling only the military can affect.

Impeccably turned out in a tailored uniform, the Comandante had a round face, a clipped moustache and the jovial disposition of the PR man. He was going to have to disappear, he apologised – he was working on the last-minute details of an Arsenale yacht show. But Signora Rigo, he said, clapping his

Number Two on the shoulder, was a very able seaman. She would show me around.

Signora Rigo didn't look like a seaman. She looked like a socialite at a cocktail party. She was dressed in a tight skirt, had dark, bouffante hair piled onto her head, and wore shiny patent-leather shoes with high, spindly heels. As soon as we stepped onto the soft earth of the Arsenale lawns I knew they were going to be trouble. But the Comandante was partly right – Signora Rigo was supremely able, at least when it came to the Arsenale's past. Immediately she was off and running, bombarding me with a rapid fire of names, dates, figures and the forgotten achievements of long-gone naval architects.

We walked away from modern buildings, past Second World War bunkers and bomb shelters, into the middle of installations centuries old. Close to the edges of stone-lined boat basins were ancient dry docks and covered boathouses. There were mills and rope-factories, warehouses and wood kilns. The further we wandered the more dilapidated grew the buildings and the longer the grass surrounding them. Signora Rigo's ankles were growing wobblier; she was stumbling about like a fresh rating on a rough sea. At the same time she was lobbing statistics – galley tonnage, sail square-metreage, cannon weights, oar lengths, mast heights, per-unit requirements in wood, tar, canvas, manila, flax-fibre, iron and copper.

It was too much to take in. Gazing around a hundred silent, disaffected acres, I tried instead to imagine the site at its most productive. More than five centuries before Britain's own revolution ever got off the ground, the Venice Arsenale was turning out ships in literally industrial quantities.

Venice, the urban historian Lewis Mumford claimed, was the first place in the world to have consciously planned for industrial production. With the development of its arsenal in the 12th century it had become 'a new type of city, based on the differentiation and zoning of urban functions'. Its name was old, a corruption of 'dar al-sin'a', the house of industry, and like many things Venetian it had been borrowed from the Arabs of the eastern Mediterranean. But the Arsenale's techniques were new. They resembled those of the modern factory complex.

On two occasions the poet Dante came to Venice and was toured through the Arsenale's noise and smoke and seeming confusion. He was so struck by it that he used images like the caulker's vats of boiling pitch for his elaboration of hell in *The Inferno*. But the production-line process was anything but confused and its unrelenting pace brought results. By the beginning of the 1400s the Arsenale was the base for 300 commercial shipping companies operating some 3,000 trading vessels. At the height of Venice's 16th-century wars with the Turks it employed 16,000 workers, almost all of them specialists, turning out fully-equipped warships at the phenomenal rate of one a day.

The rare foreigners who visited the Arsenale – its secrets were closely kept – were astounded by the assembly-line methods evolved there. One of them recorded the process by which ships were towed past a series of canal-side loading bays. From them, each ship was successively provisioned with food, drink, ammunition, sails, rope and other equipment; in the time it took a ship to reach open water it was fully equipped for a long sea voyage. If the Grand Canal was admired around the world for its leisurely elegance, the Arsenale was a byword for the organisation and industriousness that had brought Venice its dominance of the sea.

I looked around at buildings in an advanced state of decay, mortar slowly crumbling and doors hanging from hinges. What goes up must come down – even empires. Only one solid building by the water, its façade stone-carved, its triumphal doorway high and arched, recalled grander days.

'The *Bucintoro* boathouse,' said Patricia Rigo, wiping mud from her now not-so-shiny shoes. 'But it's empty – there's nothing inside. The last *Bucintoro* was stripped of its wealth by Napoleon. It finished its days as a prison-hulk, and was finally burned.' Understandably the Signora, like most Venetians, had little love for the man who'd once famously declared his role as 'an Attila to the state of Venice'.

'Napoleon didn't treat what was left of the

Venetian naval fleet much better,' Signora Rigo added. 'It was confiscated and put under French command. The French tried to invade Ireland with it. When that didn't work Napoleon sent it after the British in the Mediterranean. But he wasn't very careful with it – along with the French fleet it was sunk by Nelson at the battle of Aboukir.'

We ambled along, Signora Rigo continuing to rake me with statistics. But I was no longer listening. For a fleet that had once dictated terms across the Mediterranean its final sinking in the hands of a disdainful conqueror seemed ignoble. Perhaps such an end was inevitable in the city-state's ever-accelerating competition with bigger nations. It was easy enough to look back in hindsight – almost from the start one could see in Venice's rarely satisfied ambition her eventual dissolution. With a little imagination I could even picture the Arsenale shipyards as they long ago set about preparing the Venetian triumph that in the end was to lead to the city's profound decline.

It started in the spring of 1201 with the arrival in Venice of a small party of Frankish knights. They had an urgent request. Anxious to recapture Jerusalem, wrested from them by the Turks a decade before, the chivalry of Western Europe was in the midst of mounting yet one more Christian Crusade.

The fourth in an attempt to rid the Levant of Muslim supremacy, it wasn't a struggle for which Venice itself had ever shown much taste. Venetians were above all traders, and it was peace, not war, that was good for business. In dispute Venice preferred the subtle arts of diplomacy and negotiation, and if she fought it was usually in defence of trade, not God. On the whole buying and selling in the East meant friendly relations with local partners – as business plans go, firing boulders at Muslims with siege-catapults made little sense.

But on this Fourth Crusade the nobles of Europe were not asking the Venetians to take up arms. The Franks had a logistical problem – the transport of a vast crusading army across the Mediterranean to the Levant. And Venice was the only power with the maritime resources to do it.

Sea transport for 4,500 knights and their horses,

9,000 squires, 20,000 foot-soldiers, food and supplies for nine months … it was a massive undertaking for a small city. Its completion would require the full-time labours of 30,000 *Arsenalotti* and sailors, fully half the Republic's adult population. Yet the Venetians, under their wily Doge, Enrico Dandolo, soon enough agreed to the proposition.

Dandolo's role in the events that followed has been debated ever since. But most concur that the venerable leader was attracted by more than the exorbitant sum he demanded – 85,000 marks, twice the annual income of the French and English thrones combined. There was also the Crusaders' promise, in return for the provision of fifty Venetian galleys, of half the territories they might conquer. And if Dandolo was blind and approaching his ninetieth year, none doubt his ambition and inner vision. Some scholars believe that even from this early point he had already set his sights on the greatest prize of all – Constantinople.

Relations with the Christian empire of the East may have soured over Venetian success in Levantine markets, but to the Doge's contemporaries the idea of taking Constantinople by force was, of course, preposterous – Crusades were work done in the name of God. Venice rolled up its collective sleeves and the Arsenal laboured as it had never done before. And in a frantic year and a half the job was done. In the autumn of 1202 the Fourth Crusade assembled in Saint Mark's Basin. There were so many ships, nearly 500 of them, that the fleet stretched all the way across the lagoon to the Lido. It included an escort of fifty war galleys, 240 troopships, seventy supply ships and 120 cavalry carriers, the last equipped with flat keels and ramped hull doors for amphibious equestrian landings. For its era not even the transport of men and materiel to today's Gulf and Iraq Wars could compare to it. 'Never did finer fleet sail from any port,' wrote the proud knight Geoffrey de Villehardouin. 'Our armament could undertake the conquest of the world!'

But the fleet was in deep trouble even before it weighed anchor. For there were in fact several cities in the world which were now candidates for conquest by the Fourth Crusade. Behind the scenes there had been duplicity and double-dealing from the beginning.

The Frankish soldiers in the holds of the troop-ships had always believed they were to head directly to Jerusalem. It wasn't the case – the Crusade's leaders had judged Egypt to be the weakest point in the Arab's Middle-Eastern defences. But they had withheld revealing their intended destination in the justifiable fear that the rank-and-file would refuse any less prestigious target than the Holy City itself. As for the Venetians, they had probably never planned to land an attacking force in Egypt at all – they had recently concluded a highly lucrative trade agreement with the ruler of Egypt, and almost certainly informed him of the Crusaders' plans.

Dandolo, who despite his age and blindness sailed in splendour from the lagoon on a Venetian flagship, had drawn up for himself a wholly different itinerary. When news had leaked out before departure that the Holy Land was not the intended landfall, the disillusion was huge – fully two thirds of the fleet's compliment failed to show up in Venice. It was a mortal blow, for it meant that the self-financing Crusaders could not pay the Venetians the huge sum they'd been promised. But a deal was a deal in Venetian eyes, and the Doge now saw that he could work Crusader insolvency to his own advantage. Not far down the coast the Dalmatian city of Zara, until recently a Venetian possession, had fallen into Hungarian hands. The Doge now proposed that if *en route* the Crusaders would help him reclaim it, payment could be deferred and the Crusade proceed.

The Franks were aghast. Zara was a Christian city, and under the protection of the Pope. But Dandolo had the upper hand and, short of annulling the entire venture, there was little choice. Arriving at Zara, Franks and Venetians stormed the walls, took the city, and promptly began fighting over the spoils. Just as promptly, the Pope excommunicated the lot of them. Venice had consolidated her power in the Adriatic, but the action hardly spoke well for what was supposed to be a band of brothers, true believers embarking against a common infidel enemy.

The horizon ahead only grew darker when, just prior to sailing on from Zara, the fleet was joined by a hopeful young man, one Alexius Angelus. The son of Isaac Angelus, the former Byzantine Emperor who'd been deposed by his brother, Alexius had also cut a deal with the Doge. If the fleet escorted him to Constantinople and there assisted him to his rightful place on the throne of Byzantium, he'd agreed to show the greatest gratitude – he would pay the Crusaders 200,000 marks, supply them with 10,000 soldiers, and guarantee to protect Frankish possessions in the Holy Land. And finally, he promised, he would return the Byzantine Empire to the authority of the Catholic Church.

This was the clincher. To mend the Great Schism, the theological rift that for 150 years had irreconcilably divided Rome and Constantinople, would be an undreamed-of achievement. For apostate Crusaders who looked on the invasion of yet another Christian city with dismay, it was a moral green light. Alexius' money could pay off the Doge and finance the bankrupt force's invasion of Egypt. But the return of Constantinople to the Papal fold would buy the eternal blessings of the Pope himself.

There were other Crusaders, though, who didn't

see the opportunities offered in Constantinople in quite such a Christian way. To most soldiers in the ragtag armies that marched across the medieval world the storming of cities meant one thing only. Muslim or Christian, they held out the prospect of loot. And it was not long after the fleet rowed up the Bosphorus, dropping anchor off the walls of the Byzantine capital in June 1203, that they forced open the most splendid treasure-chest of them all.

Constantinople, Greek-speaking, Christian Orthodox and 1,800 years old, was at the time the capital of the most sophisticated civilisation on earth. Its urbane citizens had long regarded their Catholic co-religionists as primitive bumpkins. The Crusaders in turn regarded the Byzantines, long used to the luxurious ways of the East, as effete. But however sissyish they may have been, their city, many times the size of any Western capital, made Venice's magnificence pale by comparison. To the Franks gazing up at Constantinople from the decks of their ships for the first time this was the stuff of legend – a repository of classical Greek and Roman tradition, a city that had preserved Christianity amidst barbarian onslaught, and a place overflowing with unimaginable wealth.

At its heart stood the Basilica of Hagia Sophia – Holy Wisdom – a miracle of engineering far grander than any European cathedral. Yet it was just one church in a capital where there were more than a hundred others dedicated to the Virgin alone. Constantinople was a metropolis of stone-carved palaces, a city of bazaars without end. And everywhere there were statues, monuments and columns, holy relics and priceless works of art from across the ancient world.

There were wood-carvings from Troy, marbles from the Acropolis, bronzes from the foundation of Rome, copper-sheathed pillars erected by Constantine himself. There were, of course, the famous four horses of the Hippodrome, cast in an alloy whose composition had been forgotten altogether. Nor was Constantinople simply a gallery of pagan art. The legendary Crown of Thorns; the spear that pierced Christ's side; the Virgin Mary's Robe; the finger of the doubting Saint Thomas; not one, but two heads of John the Baptist – these and countless other relics were collected in the treasure house at the centre of the world.

And in that catastrophic visitation from the West it was all destroyed, a great civilisation either smashed to pieces or dispersed to the far corners of Europe. Headed by blind Dandolo himself, sword in hand, a Venetian assault led to a breaching of the sea-walls beside the Golden Horn. Constantinople was taken in a day, Isaac was hauled up from the dungeon in which he'd languished, and his son Alexius was installed beside him on the Byzantine throne. Where now, demanded the conquerors, was the promised cash?

Heavy taxes were imposed. The silver lamps of Hagia Sophia were melted down for coin. Resentment and hatred grew by the day. Payments slowed down and finally stopped. The Franks threatened retribution. The Constantinopolitans tried to set the Venetian fleet aflame. A Byzantine nobleman, determined to have done with foreigners, deposed father and son, both of whom were shortly after murdered. With the death of Alexius went the last chance of any kind of negotiated payment. The Franks decided to pay themselves.

Rape, pillage, murder and destruction – few sacks in history have measured up to the sack of Constantinople. For three days sword-wielding Crusaders, half-crazed with blood and lust and drink, rampaged about the city in a riot of wanton destruction. Whole quarters blazed. Palaces were smashed, churches stripped, libraries burned, mosaics ripped down, bronzes wrenched from their plinths. In Hagia Sophia, the holy of holies, a drunken prostitute was installed on the Patriarch's throne, where she screamed blasphemies, and 'sang bawdy songs, and danced immodestly in the holy place'. It was little wonder that the Byzantines saw the Crusaders as heralds of the Antichrist.

As the Franks were destroying what they couldn't carry off wholesale, the Venetians were far more selective in their choices – they moved calmly about the city crating up its greatest treasures. But the most valuable possession that Venice carried home from the sack of Constantinople was not gold or silver – it was dominance of the entire eastern Mediterranean.

Dandolo was perfectly happy to allow a Flemish nobleman to assume the throne in Constantinople – he knew that feudalisation and inevitable squabbling would only keep his rivals, and the Byzantine Empire itself, weak and divided. But what he did secure with great satisfaction was the foundation for the Venetian empire of the future. Assuming the poetically sonorous and topographically-correct title of 'Lord of a Quarter and Half a Quarter of the Roman Empire', Dandolo accepted the Venetian portion of the carve-up of Byzantium – Crete, the western coasts of Thrace and the Greek mainland, the Ionian islands and the Peloponnese. His agreed-upon three-eighths of the spoils were carefully chosen – it was these lands that now gave Venice an uninterrupted chain of ports from the Venetian lagoon to the Black Sea. Before Venice had been a trading city. Now it was a trading empire.

So in the end it was not German, French or Flemish knights who were the real benefactors in Constantinople. It was the power that had engineered, or at the very least facilitated, its downfall – Venice itself.

Within a few decades the empire and its capital was retaken by the Byzantines. But Venice hung on to the commercial colonies she had won, used them as a base to acquire others, and for 250 years made huge profits from them. By the end of that time Venetians had become the greatest shipbuilders, sailors and traders in the world, and their city the most beautiful in Europe.

Many European historians now say that an earlier invasion by Turks or Mongols would have been preferable to Constantinople's Christian sacking – the damage to Western heritage would have been less. They go further still, maintaining that the destruction did more than simply annihilate a great civilisation. For while the Byzantine Empire of the Greeks was to linger on, it never recovered. A strong Byzantium might have provided protection on Europe's south-eastern flank, but a weakened Byzantium was no match for Turkish armies. In 1453 the city was once again invaded, this time to become Istanbul, capital of the Ottomans. The greed that brought about the destruction of eastern Christendom by western

Christendom was to result in the Ottoman domination of much of Eastern Europe for five centuries. And Venice, inevitably in the front line through much of the conflict, was to suffer greatly for Doge Dandolo's overarching ambition.

Empires come and go, and so do conducted tours. As I'd been reflecting Signora Rigo had been directing me towards the grand gate of the Arsenale. The spate of facts and figures had nearly dried up. But oddly enough, as we reached harder ground and my guide ceased wobbling uncertainly on her heels she seemed to lose the firm confidence she had so far displayed.

Around the gate were ranged four stone-carved lions, so famous in Venice, affirmed the Signora, that erudite scholars had written entire volumes about their history and provenance. One had probably been removed from the Lion Terrace at Delos to commemorate the short-lived Venetian recapture of Corfu from the Turks in 1716. Two others had been taken from Piraeus to mark the temporary reconquest of the Peloponnese by Francesco Morosini in 1687.

But the origins of the fourth lion, my guide

had to admit as we shook hands goodbye, left her stumped.

It was an odd-looking creature. Was it Greek? Syrian? Roman? Did it celebrate a victory in Venice's centuries of straggling rear-guard actions against the Turks? Signora Rigo shrugged her shoulders. 'I just don't know,' she said. 'To tell you the truth, I believe the specialists got it wrong. To me it doesn't look like a lion at all. I think it's a dog.'

Such are the occasional uncertainties one comes across in the recounting of the Venetian past, I thought as I walked home. But of the folly of the sack of Constantinople there could be little doubt at all.

Twelve

There was an early-morning fog lying over Venice when I made my way to the church of the Friari a day or two later. In the muffled and empty medieval streets I must have circled around it two or three times, quite lost, before it loomed out of the mist before me like a brick cliffside.

It wasn't the grand Gothic entrance that I made for, but a smaller doorway on the far side of the church. When the Franciscans were in their Venetian heyday there could have been no shortage of monks to serve the Friari. Nor did they have to walk far to get there. Fifteen hundred of them were housed in the vast adjoining monastery I was now entering.

I hoped for their sake that all those bodies had generated a little warmth. Outside a humid chill in the air went right to the bones. Inside it seemed even colder. No wonder the monks had spent summer and winter in the same thick woollen robes. Seven hundred years later the building was still damp and unheated, and I wondered how the staff of the Venetian State Archives coped.

I wasn't expecting to be met by a robed and cowled abbot, but I imagined that the archival director of such a place would be something like that – no one, I was sure, could spend a more than a month or two in these gloomy corridors without becoming distinctly monkish. So when I was collected at the reception desk by the Dottoressa Alessandra Schiavon, twenty-four years in the business and still as bright and lively as the young women in Tintoretto's 'Mercury and the Three Graces', I was taken aback.

The Dottoressa was a step or two ahead of the monks. Not only did she wear a warm woollen skirt, she fought the cold radiating up from the flag-stoned paving with thick stockings and high leather boots as well. But monkish she was not. Her fingers flashed with jewellery and gold rings, her face was surrounded by a nimbus of curly dark hair, and her smile was warm and animated. It didn't seem to matter where I went – the women of Venice were vivacious and formidable. No one, surely, could deal with the cold, dead hand of history more effectively. Alessandra Schiavon loved what she did – for her the Venetian past had never stopped living at all.

The archivist led me through an arched and columned reading room, once the monastery refectory. A few scholars were already installed there, heads lowered over tomes and documents. Every day hundreds of tourists passed through the Friari next door, but here a serene calm reigned. Did non-academics ever arrive, I whispered, to disturb the peace?

'Sometimes,' the Dottoressa said as I followed her towards the heart of the monastery. 'Journalists and photographers like the Archives, although they're more interested in the setting than the documents. Occasionally we get filmmakers, too, although that doesn't always work out. The last bunch, a German documentary crew, thought things needed livening up. They tried to bring a Venetian lion onto the set – a real one.'

Passing through the monastery cloister we paused at a tall Franciscan monument, all marble saints and winged angels, that rose over the monks' well.

'Nobody in Venice much likes Napoleon, but we should be thankful he knew an opportunity when he saw it,' Signora Schiavon said as she admired the well. 'He was a record keeper himself. When he closed down the city's powerful religious orders and threw out their clerics he saw he suddenly had a space large enough to house all the republic's documents. And it had to be large. In the 8th century a Venetian widow gave thirty-five baskets of olives to a monastery in Friuli. The donation was recorded, and not much has happened since that wasn't. Deeds, wills, property purchases, marriages, inheritances, bills of sale … barely a scrap of parchment or piece of paper has been thrown away. It all ended up here.'

It sounded dreary enough to send even a conveyancer into a state of rigid catalepsy. But it wasn't really. The Venetians were thorough, systematic and secretive rulers, and public consultation was not the order of the day. The Great Council, the Senate, the Collegio, the Signoria, the Council of Ten ... the higher one climbed through the levels of power the less one knew of their deliberations. Yet like most such tightly-run organisations, the Venetian Republic had an obsessive mania for taking down and preserving its minutae. What lay inside these walls went some way beyond olive transactions – it was the most detailed record of early modern state rule in the world.

On the far side of the cloister we plunged into a confusing, multi-floored maze where windows were few and far between. In all directions lay long corridors, high-ceilinged chambers and tiny monks' cells. All were stuffed from top to bottom with paper – faded paper and folded paper; paper in boxes old and new; paper rolled into scrolls and tied with coloured ribbons; paper worm-eaten and mildewed and reeking with age. It seemed unlikely that one small city could have produced quite so many written words.

In a moment I was lost. The halls went on forever, running off into the distance like an exercise in

Renaissance artistic perspective. In an earlier age so little was known about this hidden world that rumours of the Archives were rife. They were wild estimates about how many hundred rooms it contained, how many million volumes. Jan Morris tells the story of the number-addled geographer Andrea Balbi, who calculated there were 693,176,720 pages of paper in the Archive which, if laid out one after the other, would create a trail 1,444,800,000 feet long and go eleven times around the globe.

It was all exaggeration, the Dottoressa assured me. In total there were seventy-eight kilometres of shelves in 300 rooms. Inspired by the brain-fevered Balbi, I made a quick calculation. That was a mere 255,840 linear feet of documents – hardly anything at all, really. Still, said the archivist, she could probably find something here that would interest me.

And she did. Signora Schiavon assured me no one could know the entire Archive. But as we walked through corridor after corridor she had no difficulty picking out items relating to the great *Stato del Mar*, the sea-state that was Venice.

'Water, water ... let me see,' she murmured, running her eyes over ancient document boxes. 'Yes, here we are. These are the proceedings from meetings of the *Savii ed Esecatori alle Aquae* – the Wise Men and Executors in the Ministry of Water. They were responsible for advising on water in all its states – river, lagoon or open sea. We have 1,200 boxes of theirs in this room. This one contains ... ah ... a map and directives on water control in the Venetian mainland city of Vicenza.' Suddenly I was looking at a detailed, coloured map of canals and irrigated rice-fields that the great hydraulic engineer, Leonardo da Vinci himself, might have admired.

From there we moved outward into deeper and faster-flowing waters. In scarred leather volumes we looked at a neat hand, 500 years old, that had recorded debates and disputes over navigation on the Brenta River. Miles of shelves away we pored over the inner workings of the Mercanzia, the body that regulated the finances of mercantile transport. We strolled on to look at packets of trade correspondence, listings of maritime cargoes, catalogues of anchorage fees, sailors' employment registers, customs records, edicts on the provision of shipyard timber from Dalmatian forests, insurance claims for shipwrecks, retirement regulations for master mariners, cannon production in the Arsenale. There was the daily log of the ship *Sacra Famillia* sailing to Constantinople; of the *Nova Caesarea* setting out for Alexandria; of the *Calima* beating eastward against a stiff scirocco on her way to Salonica.

After a while I began to feel quite as worn out as any struggling crew member on the *Calima*. The State Archives were exhaustive and exhausting. The Dottoressa was indefatigable, but my feet were beginning to complain. And still we hadn't covered the tiniest fraction of Mediterranean material.

What, I asked my guide, hoping the question might delay a proposed hike to over to Maritime Diplomacy on the far side of the monastery, was her own favourite topic in the Archive?

She didn't hesitate for a moment. 'Veronica Franco,' she said. 'Do you know of her?'

I shook my head.

'She was a celebrated 16th-century courtesan, a beautiful woman of strong character, famous for her affairs with Venice's greatest painters and writers. Living with poets, she became a poetess herself. She wrote excellent sonnets and verse epistles. She was an early feminist – she refused to conform to the ideal of the silent and obedient Renaissance woman. When I began reading Veronica Franco I felt an extraordinary complicity with her – it was research into her letters that got me interested in Venetian history in the first place.'

Being a woman in the Venice of the 1500s, said Signora Schiavon, especially a woman who had to live by her charms, was far from easy.

'But she was fiery and gave in to no one,' she enthused. 'Once she was insulted by Maffio Venier, a poet from a powerful and aristocratic Venetian family. She dared to stand up to him. In fact she challenged him to a three-part duel – first in bed, second in poetry and last in arms.'

Lara Croft, I thought, curl up and die.

But Veronica Franco's most celebrated bedfellow,

I learned, was not a poet, although she later wrote two sonnets for him. In 1574 Henry III of France, twenty-three years old and recently proclaimed king, arrived on a visit to Venice. It was from the first moment an extraordinary occasion. Escorted into the lagoon by fourteen galleys, he rode on a Venetian ship rowed by four hundred Slavs, sailing past triumphal arches built by Palladio and decorated by Tintoretto and Veronese. Around him was a fantasy armada – boats got up as dolphins and Neptunes and a raft upon which skilled artisans blew glass objects in a flame-breathing, dragon-shaped furnace.

Things only got more fevered from there. Henry was installed at the Ca' Foscari on the Grand Canal, sleeping in bedsheets of crimson silk and surrounded by the finest furnishings and works of art the Venetians could lay their hands on. Dinner for 3,000 guests at the Doge's palace was a sumptuous offering: 1,200 dishes on silver plate and delicate white damask serviettes that on handling turned out to be fashioned of spun sugar. After the banquet the King went to the opera, only to emerge to a naval miracle. Before dining he had been shown all the elements of a war-galley laid out before him in pieces – now the galley was fully assembled and riding the water by the quayside, its deck embellished with a 16,000-pound cannon, still hot, cast during dinner.

How could such delicious evenings not end in the company of Veronica Franco, selected by the French King himself from an album of painted miniatures thoughtfully provided by the city fathers and featuring the most acclaimed prostitutes of Venice? It is said that after his visit Henry returned home in a somewhat fuddled state of mind; despite all the luxuries and romances the French court offered he spent the rest of his life quite overwhelmed by Venice.

Henry's visit left almost as indelible a mark on Venice itself. For the occasion was an exception, a moment's happy and carefree celebration in an age in which dire writing had been on the wall for some time. By the 1400s Venice had reached her apogee. She was to live on for another three centuries – in fact as her power and influence dwindled in the world she main-tained a pretence at home with ever more splendid balls, masques and decadent revels. But her long decline was there for everyone to see. Usually it was characterised by a steady nibbling away by the Turks at her Mediterranean possessions. But occasionally it was marked by sudden revelations of catastrophe. One such disclosure lay in the shelves of diplomatic correspondence on the far side of the monastery.

We got there some time around midday after an arduous slog. I trailed down one corridor after another behind the energetic Dotoressa, wishing there was a faster, more convenient route. By this point I would have said yes to an electric wheelchair, a Smart Car or any other modern vehicle that could have negotiated these halls. But my guide would not have approved. As she was about to show me, innovations in transport can sometimes have disastrous aftermaths.

In 1499, seventy-five years before Veronica Franco was to fête Henry III, appalling news arrived in diplomatic letters from King Manuel's court in Lisbon. A Portuguese sea captain, Vasco da Gama, had travelled to India and back via the southern tip of Africa.

It took some years for the full weight of the disaster

to penetrate Venetian minds. After all, another Portuguese, Bartholemew Diaz, had already rounded the Cape of Good Hope. But more farsighted men at the Rialto could see that a successful sea trip to India and back spelt ruin. It meant nothing less than the end of Venetian global trading supremacy.

For no longer would Oriental silks and spices have to be carried thousands of miles on horse- or camel-back across the trading routes of Central Asia. Nor would water-born cargoes from the East have to be trans-shipped – unloaded in Suez or the Persian Gulf, carried overland and then reloaded in Levantine ports. Goods could now travel in a single vessel, bypassing the Venetian-controlled eastern Mediterranean altogether. If they were headed towards the rich markets of northern Europe – Holland, England or the Hanseatic ports – they didn't have to enter the Mediterranean at all. Lisbon, not Venice, would now become Europe's entrepôt for eastern goods. The Middle Sea was no longer vital to European commerce. In one stroke da Gama had transformed the Mediterranean into a backwater.

Foreign technology was partly to blame for

Venice's suddenly diminished prospects. Challenged by a vast, unknown ocean, the nations of Atlantic Europe had developed better ships, more advanced navigation techniques, more highly skilled sailors. Venice, born to the sea, had finally been outperformed in her own liquid element.

But in the larger view her out-classing was part of a more important global shift. It was an historic change that moved the entire centre of the world's human gravity north-westwards. The Mediterranean, so long the principle stage of European civilisation, was no longer to be the focus of the Western world. There were new economic forces at work, new political ideologies forming, new social classes emerging. And they took shape on the shores of that other, larger body of water, the Atlantic.

In a short time the silver pouring eastwards from the recently discovered Americas would make Venice's wealth look paltry. It would turn Spain into the superpower of the West, and make her the main rival to that superpower of the East, the Ottoman Empire. Out-performed by both, Venice was destined to become an irrelevance, a charming but powerless anachronism: she would end up one of the first tourist-curiosities in the world, a place where pleasure came ahead of any other business.

It was my own pleasure, after the morning's exertions, to sit and chat for a few minutes. Before she left me Alessandra Schiavon took me up to a small office under the monastery roofs and sat me before a diminutive woman in her eighties. Grey-haired, dressed in warm, tweedy clothes, Maria Francesca Tiepolo had passed the morning hours working on the Latin text that lay on her desk.

The elderly Signora had, in fact, spent an entire lifetime unravelling the secrets of Venice – an employee of the State Archives for three decades, she had for her last thirteen years been its Director. And now in her retirement she continued research on her favourite subjects. I asked about her name. It was one of the most famous in Venetian history, belonging to a family that produced admirals, governors, aristo-cratic conspirators, dukes of Crete and two celebrated 13th-century doges.

The Signora modestly admitted that she counted Doge Lorenzo Tiepolo among her direct forbears. History lives on everywhere in Venice, she said. It is in its old papers, in its monuments and palaces and paintings, and in its people, too. Time, she said, is a continuous flow connecting everything. And as I watched her talk, her eyes bright, her smile warm and strong, I had the curious feeling that I might have been watching the Dottoressa forty years on in the future. Or looking at Veronica Franco 400 years ago.

It was an eerie sensation, and it pursued me back down the long monastery corridors and across the silent refectory. Then I was through the tall doors of the Archives and away from the damp world of paper secrets. And suddenly it was hard to believe that time, for all its connective power, could even join the two halves of a day. For outside the thick fog of morning had vanished. It might never have existed at all, and the great brick façade of the Friari lay basking in a warm and dazzling afternoon sun.

Thirteen

Il Moro de Venezia II – the Moor of Venice – sat docked at a quayside directly in front of the *Bucintoro* boathouse. It was as if by simple proximity alone, by rubbing herself against stones where the older boat must have often tied up, she might appropriate to herself some of the same prestige and grandeur. I was no expert in multi-million dollar high-tech racing yachts, but as I sat there waiting she looked pretty grand anyway.

I had returned to the Arsenale to rendezvous with Maurizio Vecchiola, scion of the family who owned the *Moro*. The Vecchiolas were not just simple sailing folk – they also owned one of the largest industrial PVC manufacturing firms in the world. But the *Moro* was their pride and joy. The yacht was, by all accounts, a well-known international racer, although she wouldn't be racing today. Instead she would be overseeing a different kind of race, a regatta of traditional wooden sailing boats organised by the Venice yacht club, the Compagnia della Vela. The *Moro* would merely be lending a little mystique to the event.

Already on board were the *Moro*'s skipper and mate. When the yacht was in full racing fettle she required a crew of twenty-two energetic young men, experts who flew at stainless steel winch handles like furies and counted time lost in microseconds. But even out of season, laid up and inactive, the *Moro* had its skeleton crew – you don't leave a million-dollar baby without a nanny. We introduced ourselves and the pair got on with loading the largest canvas sacks I'd ever seen. The *Moro* carried enough sail to fit out a small armada.

A small knot of men came striding down the grassy path where Patrizia Rigo had wobbled a few days before. They were no more naval officers than she was. I doubted they were yacht club officials, either. Unshaven, wearing black clothes and dark sunglasses, they looked more like a Mafia hit-squad. They turned out instead to be Gucci men. The Vecchiola family sold PVC to Gucci for the making of Gucci shoe-soles. Men of lesser vision might entertain esteemed associates in corporate hospitality tents at public sporting events. Maurizio Vecchiola, for his part, had a floating hospitality tent that provided its own sport. Having sustained the indignity of an inspection of their own footwear by the *Moro*'s crew – no ordinary street-soles ever touched the boat's fabulous Kevlar-carbon composite deck – the Gucci shoe men sat around looking fashionably bored.

Another party approached, looking much more like sailors. It was Corrado Scrascia, the official from the Compania della Vela, and his little team of yacht-club officials, judges and timekeepers. Signor Scrascia was no Gucci man. No one bothered to glance at his shoes. From the white smile in his tanned face to the buttons on his multi-function chronometer he looked every bit a saltwater yachtsman.

The team with him also looked nautical. They had brought along orange marker buoys, aerosol-powered starting horns and a whole boxful of folded signal-flags you had to be a sailor to understand. They began preparing the *pilotina*, the little outboard motor-boat tied behind the *Moro*'s stern, that would accompany the race along its course.

Finally Maurizio Vecchiola turned up. He didn't look like a sailor at all. He looked like a kid out of a private prep school. But his responsibilities were large, he told me – his father had put him in charge of the company's North American operations, a large and expanding chunk of the business. Still, I found it a challenge to associate the young Vecchiola with either competitive yacht racing or cutthroat corporate business. He wore nerdy glasses, loafers with tassels and a bespoke button-down blue shirt whose tail hung out of the back of his trousers. In fact he did little sailing that day. His main function was to entertain.

The white wine secured, the cocktail sausages safely stowed away, we started the engines and cast off. The marine approaches to Venice are busy. Once outside the Arsenale basin we motored through the thick of weekend traffic, small craft going in all directions in an unrelenting flow. There were sleek speedboats with curvaceous young women perched on their bows like exotic car hood-ornaments; small sailing dinghies with parents and children plump in bright life-vests; wide, multi-decked car-carriers piggybacking vehicles from the mainland to the roads of the Lido; sightseeing tour-boats of the Azienda del Consorzio Trasporti Veneziano, operators of the city's *vaporetto* services. But for sheer size the most impressive boats were the international ferries running the Adriatic routes southwards to Greece. Ten stories high, they reared sheer out of the water in front of us like giant icebergs. From the sundeck of the *Ikarus Palace*, escorted out of port by two black and white tugs and bound for Patras, tiny figures gazed down and waved. All of us, the Gucci men excepted, waved back.

'Welcome aboard,' said Maurizio Vecchiola as the *Moro* veered to port, entering a busy navigation channel leading towards the barrier island of the Lido. 'The first thing you should know is that the *Moro* is one of the most important boats in the world.'

'You must tell me why,' I said as he indicated a free place beside him in the cockpit. But I knew he was not going to need any encouragement.

The technical explanations that followed were complex, and I won't pretend I understood them. Suffice to say it was impressed upon me that the *Moro* was a member of that elite and blue-blooded caste of yachts, the Maxi-I.O.R. I had never heard of them. The International Offshore Rule that defined this class of boat in fact no longer pertained and Maxis were no longer being built. More confusing still, other changes of rule meant that the *Moro* was now considered a 'Mini-Maxi'. To me the boat was sounding more and more like some kind of revolutionary new sanitary pad. But no matter – at seventy-one feet long, she was among the fastest, costliest and, above all, largest racing yachts ever designed. It was craft like this that had brought international renown to such races as the Fastnet, the Sydney-to-Hobart and the America's Cup.

The *Moro* was now twenty-two years old, Vecchiola told me, and no longer the innovative racing craft she had once been. But that was not the point. The point was that she was a noble boat with noble owners who had made a place for her in yachting history. In fact the list of personalities associated with the *Moro* over the years seemed more important to Vecchiola than the yacht herself.

She'd been owned by the greatest captains of Italian industry. She was designed and built for Raul Gardini, agro-chemical industrialist, once owner of the second biggest corporation in Italy, and the yachtsman who'd put Italy on the international racing map. Later, among other illustrious owners, she'd also belonged to Carlo De Benedetti, then head of the Olivetti Corporation.

The names rang a bell. Hadn't Raul Gardini committed suicide in a notorious financial corruption case in the 1990s? If it came to that, hadn't Carlo De Benedetti also been brought low in a series of Italian kickback scandals? But there was no time for questions. Vecchiola Junior had moved on to Dennis Conner, the yachtsman who'd won the America's Cup back for America. He, too, had sailed the *Moro*. Why, even royalty, in the person of King Juan Carlos of Spain, had skippered this boat. And, in a way, the circle had now been completed – the Vecchiolas bought the raw materials for their PCV from the Porto Marghera chemical factory across the lagoon that had once been owned by Raul Gardini. It really was a return to the source, wasn't it?

I had to agree it was. What else could I say? By this point I was drinking the man's wine and nibbling his canapés. But Maurizio Vecchiola's bedazzlement by the great and the good of the yachting world was rather worrisome – nobody that young should be so impressed by status and money. What was really worrying me at this point, though, wasn't yachts at all, but wind. There wasn't a breath of it, either for the *Moro* or the little flotilla of aged craft we were now slowly approaching.

They were beautiful old boats, cutters for the most part, some of them built close to a century ago. Lovingly maintained, their long bowsprits and wooden hulls glowed beneath multiple layers of varnish. For the moment they looked rather sorry, their rust-coloured sails hanging limp as they waited in a small knot on the still, glassy water. Until a minute or two before we had been in the lagoon, motoring behind the protected lee of the Lido. But now we had cleared its north end through the Porto di Lido – the main passage to and from Venice – and sailed out into the open Adriatic. And still there was no wind.

Signor Scrascia called his men together at the stern of the *Moro*. They searched the heavens, gazed at the horizon, sniffed the air. After lengthy deliberation they issued their verdict: we would hang on. Given their reading of the skies, to say nothing of the weather forecast printed in the day's local paper, there was every chance that an afternoon wind would eventually pick up. We would just have to be patient.

And so we sat. Tillers hard over, the antique boats floated nearby, drifting slowly in desultory little circles. Bored by the seafaring life, the Gucci men banded together over a second bottle of wine and got down to Milanese fashion gossip. Corrado Scrascia strung a taut cord between two mast-stays and hung up a series of signal flags with clothes-pegs. It looked like an especially colourful laundry line, but apparently informed the world at large that the old-boats regatta was on hold. Signor Scrascia's men jumped into the *pilotina* to lay out buoys marking the regatta's course. Maurizio Vecchiola conferred with his father on his mobile telephone, then joined the men in black to regale them with stories of shoes and the sea. I sat down, my feet hanging over the bow, and gazed out over the water.

Not far away stretched the groomed beaches of the Lido, so close I could see long rows of bathing cabins and regularly laid out beach umbrellas. It was too early in the year for anyone to be using them. Behind loomed the bulky Palazzo del Cinema. It was there that every summer for seventy years the prestigious Venice Film Festival was celebrated. But in my mind's eye I was already picturing another annual event. It had been held for a good deal longer, was even more prestigious, and in its way was just as cinematic. It was here, on the very spot where we were floating, that for 800 years Venice had celebrated her Marriage to the Sea.

It had begun with nothing more than a naval campaign against piracy, a scourge that had troubled shipping in Mediterranean waters for centuries. On Ascension Day in the year 1000 Doge Pietro Orseolo II sailed out of the lagoon to rid the Adriatic of some particularly troublesome Croatians. His pacification programme went well – when he returned the sea was a Venetian sea, amenable to the establishment of commercial outposts, trade and profitable voyages. To commemorate the event a yearly Ascension Day celebration was organised. Led by the Doge in the bows of the *Bucintoro*, the churchmen and the people of Venice sailed out to the Porto di Lido in a great decorated fleet for a service of invocation.

At first things remained simple – a short prayer of thanks was followed by the singing of psalms. But the Venetians, ever in love with spectacle, were not ones to let such a dramatic opportunity pass them by. As time went on a simple act of propitiation – the Doge's casting of a gold ring into the sea – began to invest the ritual with overtones of matrimony. In a short while the service, a 'sign of our true and perpetual dominion' over the waves, became a full blown *Spos-alazio del Mar*, a symbolic marriage of the city to the sea.

Only the Venetians could pull off such a spiritual union with the pomp, style and extravagance it merited. And only the Venetians, with their eye for material value, could encourage such a hasty recuperation of their marital investment. There was no hoard of 800 gold wedding rings lying on the shallow sea-bed beneath our keel. At the end of each ceremony, Venitian citizens were free to dive in and look for the ring. Not only was it 'finders keepers' – the successful diver was exempted from all taxes and state obligations for a year.

An hour passed, then another. I was enjoying the soft light, the low green islands off in the lagoon, the tall campaniles of Venice rising above the Lido. The Gucci men were less happy and rapidly growing mutinous. Corrado Scrascia could only smile politely at their impatience as we bobbed about direction-less. Just as I was deciding it was all over I felt the faintest hint of cool air on my cheek. We all felt it.

Even Maurizio Vecchiola, crestfallen at the prospect of a public-relations failure, perked up. Stronger by the minute, the wind was soon blowing steadily.

Signor Scrascia changed the colours on his signals line. The skipper and his mate hauled sails up onto the *Moro*'s deck. The old cutters, their own canvas now taut, positioned themselves as the aerosol horn sounded a series of race-start warnings. Then they were off.

They were only a tiny armada of fragile old leisure boats. But as they set a course south, small bow waves pushing up at their prows, I transformed them into another, more formidable flotilla of wood and canvas. Growing ever smaller in the distance, they became the Venetian warships that once sailed out past the Lido to rendezvous with other ships of a 'Holy League' that included Spain and the Papacy. Two hundred war galleys strong, this was the giant fleet that in 1571 took on an equally large Turkish armada in the Gulf of Patras off Greece. The battle of Lepanto was the largest naval action since Caesar Augustus had destroyed Anthony and Cleopatra's fleet at Actium

1,500 years earlier, and the last major engagement to be fought with oared galleys.

The writer Miguel de Cervantes, serving aboard a Spanish ship, was thoroughly impressed; not even three wounds and the loss of the use of his left hand – 'to the greater glory of the right', as he wrote – could dampen his enthusiasm. For him Lepanto was simply 'the greatest occasion that past or present ages have witnessed'. Certainly the figures were impressive: in sinkings and hand-to-hand fighting 30,000 Turks were killed, 8,000 were captured, 113 Turkish galleys were destroyed and 15,000 Christian galley slaves freed. But if the battle was counted as an unqualified triumph – the coalition itself lost a mere 15,000 men – the Holy League was really only tilting at windmills. More vigorous than ever, the Turkish navy immediately began building an even larger fleet. In the end Lepanto did little to halt Venice's long decline in the eastern Mediterranean.

Having taken time to raise its sails, the *Moro* was now gaining on the wooden boats and once again I could see them clearly. There was no sign of shot or shell in their hulls. They were no bodies floating in the water behind them. Nor did it really matter who won their competition – the wind itself was triumph enough. With the *pilotina* following closely in their wake, the *Moro* was now free to take on the wind herself. Ratchets purred, winch cogs turned on precision-fitted bearings, and a spinnaker rose high into the air. Looking up, I could see the vast face of a Venetian lion ballooning on the canvas spread above us.

The deck heeled over. Nine knots was no great speed for the Moor of Venice. I don't doubt that even a Turkish galley, given a little extra effort by a few hundred galley slaves, could have outpaced us. But soon we had left the little fleet far behind, and were rushing forward on our own. I was exhilarated. The Gucci men were exhilarated. Even Maurizo Vecchiola appeared to be enjoying not just the way the *Moro* made him look, but the way she looked herself. Proud Venetians, we might have been sailing to Byzantium.

Fourteen

It was a sunny Sunday afternoon and I hadn't been waiting more than two minutes on the Fondamenta Nuove before Umberto Sichiro hove into view, right on time.

He arrived in that most patrician of Venetian water craft, a *motoscafo*. Its superstructure gleamed white and the teakwood planking of its hull was buffed to a high sheen. Even the august figure standing in the motor launch's cabin, his shirt crisply laundered and suit freshly pressed, had a costly look about him. He wasn't Umberto Sichiro. He was the water-taxi's chauffeur, but if he hadn't been holding the pilot wheel in his hands I would have taken him for a visiting merchant banker. Given the hourly rates that Venetian launches charge he might as well have been.

The lagoon's annual Mestre Regatta was a popular event, an affair of ordinary people celebrating simple working life. But that was no reason for its contingent of Venetian journalists to show up in a boat any less well turned out than they themselves.

There were four or five photographers and reporters from local papers ensconced in the launch's plush cabin. Lounging about in marine décor – upholstered white armchairs and settee, navy blue carpet, mahogany trim – they suggested a Venetian version of those bored and sophisticated Roman *ragazzi*, the press-pack in *La Dolce Vita*.

Being not just a senior journalist but a member of the regatta's organising committee, Umberto Sichiro stood slightly apart from his younger colleagues. He remained on the *motoscafo*'s rear deck, feet planted wide in the manner of an experienced sailor, chatting to a pretty female committee member. His sunglasses were expensive, his tan shoes highly polished. Only the tie beneath the dark blue windbreaker hinted at any nautical bent – in discrete miniature it featured the same marine signals that Corrado Scracia was fond of flying. But Umberto Sichiro obviously had more than nautical charm – he had the allure and seductive manner of a middle-aged man who still attracted women. Despite his years his hair was sleek and dark. His smile was self-confident, his moustache neatly trimmed, his gestures practised. Not many people can make smoking look attractive these days, but Umberto Sichiro could. An elegant Latin sophisticate, he had all the smoothness of Mastroianni himself.

The launch touched the quay just long enough for me to hop aboard, then headed down the channel past San Michele towards Murano. I preferred to stay outside on the deck, too, not just for a better view of the race we were going to follow, but to hear what my host had to say about it.

Halfway between the two islands a couple of hundred small outboard motorboats milled noisily about nine other boats that sat calmly, waiting, with no motors at all. They were powered instead by seven rowers apiece, three on each side and one astern. The boats they manned were *caorlinas*, lumbering, flat-bottomed vessels that used to bring fruit and vegetables from the farming islands of the lagoon to Venice. To innocents like me they were simply old work boats, an awkward means of heavy transport whose day had come and gone. But to experts like Umberto Sichiro such craft were objects of complex and unending appeal. For all his Venetian sophistication Signor Sichiro was passionate about Venetian rowing craft. He had studied them all his life, and in the end I wondered if in their nuanced subtlety they were not more delectable to him than Venetian women themselves. From the slim and delicate *pupparin* to the generous, wide-hipped *sampierotta*, there wasn't an oared craft in the entire lagoon the man did not venerate.

The press launch nosed its way through the buzzing, expectant crowd floating on the water to take up its official position beside the *caorlinas*. My host cast a practised, calculating eye over the crews, and those who saw him waved and smiled. Everyone knew Umberto Sichiro.

'It's a good crowd today,' he said with satisfaction. 'These events attract all sorts of people. The contestants are mostly gondoliers and fisherman, so they draw other gondoliers and fishermen. Look at all the women and children, too – some of them are the rower's friends and families. If the rowers have rowed before and performed well, they are neighbourhood heroes – the whole quarter turns out to see them.'

I looked at the rowers standing relaxed and happy in their boats. All wore striped jerseys, red waist sashes and white trousers rolled up to the knee. They also wore the racing colours of their boats, bright primal splashes that gave the gathering the festive look of a land-bound race-meet. But these racers didn't have the physiques of jockeys – under the finery they were large, weathered, brawny men who had spent most of their lives in outdoor work.

'They have to be strong,' Umberto said, as if reading my thoughts. 'Those boats are heavy. They curve up nicely at bow at stern, but they are eleven metres long and broad across the beam.'

He held up his hand and tested the air. From out of the south-east, where a mass of dark cloud troubled an otherwise clear sky, a strong breeze was blowing up the Adriatic. 'Today physical strength is going to be especially important. On other days technique might count for more. But that wind is blowing across the *caorlina*s' bows. The last rower, the steersman, is going to have to expend some of his energy keeping his boat on a straight course. It can make all the difference. It's the compensating strength of the forward rowers which will count most.'

The course ahead was cleared, a rope was stretched over the water to form a starting line, and for a moment everything – the crowd, their boats, the rowers themselves – was still. Then a horn sounded and the rowers heaved into action. Blue lights on police boats flashed, sirens on fire boats wailed, and the whole flotilla sprang to life, moving ahead with the *caorlinas* at a steady seven knots.

Seven knots might not sound like much of a speed, but anyone who has watched the exertion of *caorlina* rowers will tell you it is positively hair-raising. Mediterranean rowers, of course, are not like northern rowers. They do not sit with their backs to their destination and put their power into pulling on oars. It is a position they find illogical. They prefer to face forward, standing upright, and put their energy into pushing on oars instead. Their outside legs ahead, their whole weight pivoting on their front feet, the *caorlina* rowers came down on each forward push with a terrific surge of muscle power. It was a demanding, synchronised rhythm they would maintain unrelentingly for the next three and three-quarter miles.

For the moment there was no apparent difference in the relative strength of the rowers. Could he, I asked the expert, predict any winners? Did he have any favourites?

Umberto looked at the boats racing over the water, then without hesitation delivered his verdict.

'The blue team will win,' he said, as if there wasn't room for the shadow of a doubt. 'Orange will come in second, pink third and violet fourth.'

'Really?' I said, surprised at the assurance in his voice. 'You can be that certain?'

'Of course,' he replied, as if he were the coach and personal trainer of each rower present. 'It is only a question of scientific knowledge. I know the technique and strength of all of them.'

That didn't stop other spectators from worrying about who might win and lose. Everyone was shouting, but from a motorboat some way behind us came an incessant, bull-like roar. A middle-aged woman wearing an orange armband was shouting so hard and heaving about so uncontrollably she was being held back in the boat by two other women.

'That's Igor Vignotto's mother,' said Umberto. 'She tends to get emotionally over-excited. It is unnecessary. Igor's a good, steady rower, very scientific.'

Apart from the rowers there was other science here I didn't understand at all. Why the need, I asked Umberto, for that grotesquely twisted bit of wood, full of strange angles and concavities, when a simple single-position, English-style oarlock would do?

'Ah,' he replied. 'The *forcola*, a most interesting piece of equipment. An oarlock couldn't possibly do the same job. You cannot even begin to row properly unless you understand the principles of the *forcola*.'

He took out a piece of paper, and using the pitching

top of the launch's cabin as a desk began drawing a series of diagrams. They were complex, schematic plans with arrows running in different directions and points labelled '*fuerza*,' '*fulcro*' and '*resistenza*'. I think they were meant to show what happens when a given impetus, augmented and redirected through leverage on a fulcrum, encounters a natural field of resistance like water. But did that mean that by slotting the oar into a higher position on the *forcola* it gave the rower more manoeuvrability but less power? Or did it provide less manoeuvrability and greater power? I was confused. I have kept the diagrams, and from time to time even study them, but they haven't become any less puzzling.

I quickly gave up trying to understand things on paper, for out on the water things were taking shape. As predicted, Celeste, the blue team, had taken the lead and was looking strong. Rosa, the pink crew, was not far behind. To Signora Vignotto's partial satisfaction Igor was giving it everything he had – Arancio, the orange team, was running a close third. But the distances between boats were gradually widening

– after fifteen minutes of vigorous rowing the lead boat was more than a hundred yards ahead of Rosso, the red team that lagged last.

By now we had left Murano far behind and were running parallel to the elevated railway-track that crosses the lagoon. Straight ahead of us lay Mestre, the industrial town that sits on its shores. After weeks spent in the confines of the lagoon such things as smokestacks, motorways and concrete blocks of workers' flats looked oddly foreign. I had almost forgotten their existence. But there they all were, looming before us. In a little while I would have to face them straight on. For the moment I was perfectly happy to see them from a boat pitching and yawing in the confused wakes of a hundred other boats.

The flotilla wasn't more than a couple of minutes from the finish-line at the San Giuliano bridge when Signora Vignotta roared especially loudly. The Oranges had called on their last reserves of strength and pulled up level with the Pinks for second place. Water streamed from oars, bodies rocked furiously, the crowds cheered their favourites hoarsely on. For a moment it seemed uncertain. Then, of course, Orange pulled slowly ahead. Umberto Sichiro smiled with pride, as if it were he himself who had won the race. Blue crossed the line first, followed by orange, pink and violet. His prediction was spot on.

'*Mamma Mia! Che spettacolo!*' the master of ceremonies kept repeating at the prize-giving on the quayside fifteen minutes later.

'*Mamma Mia! Mamma Mia!*' said my host, rolling his eyes as we stood watching winner after winner come forward to receive his award and be loudly cheered. 'Our announcer has had too much to drink again.'

Umberto was enjoying the sight of champion rowers being photographed with girlfriends, babies and proud mothers. He applauded judges long and loudly, praised organisers and time-keepers for their unstinting contributions. But towards the end it seemed to me he was becoming slightly impatient, anxious to wind up the official ceremonies. It was only half an hour afterwards, at tables set up in the garden outside the San Giuliano boating clubhouse,

ENEZIA JB₀₂

that I discovered the unofficial ceremonies the organisers had organised for themselves.

I had wandered off to look at the *caorlinas* and by the time I arrived a feast was in full swing. Up and down the tables there were tubs of small red fried fish, sardines grilled over charcoal, and *sarde in saor*, a Venetian specialty of sardines marinated in onions, wine, raisins and pine nuts. Everybody, even the most elegant of race-committee ladies, was enjoying slumming – jewellery and gold rings flashing, they ate fried fish with oily fingers, bit the heads off sardines with their teeth, and reached over their neighbour's plates for the wine.

This last item, especially, was popular. It was drunk from plastic glasses and disappeared down thirsty throats in surprising quantities. I had never seen Venetians, generally so reserved and well ordered, quite so unbuttoned. In no time they were laughing loudly, calling for more bottles and singing boat songs. They were executed in three-part harmony – this *was* Venice, after all – but they were relaxed and joyous just the same. And in the middle of it all, suavely dominating the tables with charm and elegant discourse, was Umberto Sichiro.

The songs were about rowing and so, inevitably, was the conversation. There are one 120 boat regattas in Venice each year, most of them celebrating rowing, so there was plenty to talk about. Racing techniques old and new; the exploits of former champions; the precise specifications of the two-man racing *gondolino* – all came under review. But simply talking boats was not enough. When someone from the local rowing club suggested we inspect a boat being built in the workshop next door, there was a general emptying of tables.

We crowded into a room that smelled of glue and fresh wood shavings, an odour to which we added our own winey exhalations. The boat we surrounded was far from finished and the structure of its hull, a complex series of delicate, arched ribs, still lay exposed. Tapering evenly away towards either extremity, they formed part of a perfect, diminishing geometry. The joins were flush, the angles precise, the wood sanded to a satin finish.

This was both art and science, a work of love exactingly executed.

To me it was a beautiful thing. To everyone else, too. There were low whistles, murmurs of approval, expressions of admiration. And then there was a grunt, loud and monosyllabic and disdainful, that unmistakably signified the opposite.

It came from a shambling bear of a man in a sleeveless down jacket. I had seen him officiating at the start of the *caorlina* race, and wondered who he was then. He was squat and powerfully built. Grey hair straggled down a massive head into an unkempt beard. His hands were large and rough, his blunt fingers stained with varnish. He had a kind of raw, animal force you couldn't ignore. Without his saying a word, the room had fallen silent.

'That's Gianfranco Vianello,' Umberto whispered to me over his shoulder. 'He looks primitive, but he is intelligent. Watch.'

And so I watched. Gianfranco Vianello, son of a gondolier, master boatbuilder and legendary twelve-times winner of the Regatta Storico, the greatest rowing race of all, was hard not to watch. The conversation that followed was too fast and excited for me to follow, but you didn't have to speak Italian to get the drift of things. Vianello clearly disapproved of the boat before him.

He glanced up and down its elegant lines. The construction was OK, he admitted. That wasn't the problem. The boat failed to respect the rules and style of Venetian *tradizione*.

Perhaps it didn't have to, some brave soul emboldened by wine ventured to remark; it was a handsome craft none the less, and superbly built.

The effect on Vianello was remarkable. He flushed red, clenching his fists at his side. I thought he was going to hit someone. Instead he launched into a tirade, talking louder and faster by the second. Words like *'capriccioso,' 'fantasia,' 'innovazione'* came and went in a flash. It was like a dam bursting. In a minute he was joined by a conservative supporter or two. Then, able to address someone apart from the formidable Vianello, proponents of innovation weighed in. Soon everyone had jumped into the fray and the whole room was arguing furiously about change and tradition. '*Calma*! *Calma*!' shouted Umberto, doing his best to control tempers and keep things constructive. But not even he could get a word in.

I thought Vianello was drunk. Later, I visited his workshop on Guidecca, watched him building a gondola, and realised he'd been stone-cold sober. He hadn't been purposely provocative – he was always like that. He was a force of nature, and passionate about boats.

It was difficult to explain rowing to a non-rower, Vianello told me in Guidecca as he took a break from placing ribs in a new hull. It was very personal, something to do with harmony of movement. Perhaps boxers and dancers felt the same way. But for him it was enough that he was a Venetian, and attached to the old ways of doing things. If he had to build deeper gondola hulls to take today's increased motor turbulence into account, so be it. Otherwise why not stick to the way things should be? Vianello might not have looked like a philosopher, but he struck me as being a bit like Plato. Peacefully floating somewhere in his mind were the ideal forms of every worthwhile boat that had ever been designed, built or rowed. They were perfect, eternal, immutable and unchanging. And every last one of them, of course, was Venetian.

But if Gianfranco Vianello had been in total control on the evening of the *caorlina* race, the rest of us definitely hadn't. We had all overdone it with the Friuli white.

'Never mind,' Umberto said when the last boat song was sung, the last plastic glass emptied. 'It's not far home – just over the bridge. I've got a lift for us.'

Joining two other companions, we stumbled over to a parking lot and the smallest vehicle that has ever carried four inebriated, full-sized adults over the lagoon to Venice – a baby-blue, 1960 Porsche sports-car in mint condition.

'We'll never get in,' I protested as its owner opened miniature doors and Umberto proceeded to fold himself into a back seat two feet wide and a foot deep.

Umberto replied with a kind of enthusiastic gurgle. I think he was saying it was no problem at all, but the roof of the car was so low his chin was jammed into his collarbone. Eventually I, too, got myself bent into the back seat. The driver and his other passenger installed themselves, and off we roared.

Their cramped state did not discourage the passengers of the baby-blue Porsche from picking up the debate where it had been left off before the Vianello incident. It had to do with alternate rowing stances, and which ones were most effective on heavier, slower lagoon boats. But the theme didn't discourage the driver from his keen Italian racing-style. Up on the causeway high above the water we were shooting in and out of lanes and passing everything in sight. I closed my eyes and wondered what would happen if we crashed through the barrier and headed to the bottom of the lagoon. Would take it us as long to get out of the Porsche as it had to get in?

Barely two miles separate Venice from the mainland, but it seemed a lot further to me. Umberto argued rowing all the way. When we parked and he'd finally managed to extricate himself from the back seat, he immediately took up a graceful stance and began demonstrating his alternate rowing stroke.

The other two gathered about, one criticising, one approving. Then they took up other stances to demonstrate their own preferred styles. All in all they looked pretty silly, without oars or any other props, rowing away up there on the fourth floor of the Tronchetto multi-storey car park.

I might have stayed on to debate pros and cons, too, but I had an early start the next morning. Besides, the weather had grown threatening. The wind that had been blowing up the Adriatic all afternoon had finally brought black clouds over Venice. They opened up as I scurried home, and by the time I was standing at our door in Cannaregio I was soaked.

I towelled off, refused the dinner that Jany had cooked, and was soon in bed. But I found it difficult to get to sleep that evening. I had eaten and drunk too much. Besides, I simply couldn't figure out how Umberto Sichiro had managed to predict the first four *caorlinas* over the line. It wasn't science at all. It was downright uncanny. In the end, I decided before I drifted off, you just had to be Venetian, an oarsman from the start.

Fifteen

The Adriatic rain, once it started, didn't know how to stop. It fell heavily all night, and when I got up at 5.30 to go to work it was still coming down. The wind was strong and gusty. Hunched into the weather on the Strada Nuova in the grim half-light of dawn, the few early pedestrians already on their way to work were battling with umbrellas. Two minutes from the apartment my own umbrella promptly turned inside out. Having no other wet-weather gear, I returned home and asked Jany to help me out. Half an hour later I met my Barich Trasporti co-workers at Tronchetto wearing a green plastic garbage bag with holes cut out for my arms and head.

Tronchetto lies at the working end of Venice and is not terribly chic, so I didn't feel too embarrassed

– it wasn't as if the men from Gucci were skulking about on the quays there at six o'clock on a wet Monday morning. But it was surprising how many other people were. Apart from harbouring the city's road, rail and ferry terminals, Tronchetto is the site where all mainland merchandise destined for the city is trans-shipped from trucks to delivery boats. The place was crawling.

Like a pontoon bridge leading nowhere, the Barich fleet, five boats painted in the company colours of red and black, were tied gunwale to gunwale not far past the Venice wholesale market. On either side on the busy quay other transport companies had their own *topo*s similarly moored to allow everyone a place. Crews in bright waterproof jackets and pants swarmed across rain-soaked decks. Some were loading wine and beer. The men of Soligo Dairy Products were stowing crates of yoghurt in their refrigerated *topo*s. The employees of the Merlini frozen fish company were packing cod and calamari into their own cold-storage hulls. Bananas in soggy cardboard boxes, wooden flats of green peppers, trays of aubergines glistening with drops of rainwater, all were being passed from hand to hand and carefully stacked on boat decks.

There were other items that couldn't be loaded by hand at all. Weighty acetylene welding tanks had to be lowered into a *topo* with chains and winches. A wooden spool of heavy-duty electrical cable six feet high required the ministrations of a quay-side crane. Bulk-liquid transport presented a whole other set of problems: when a sewage carrier, having filled its hold at some Venetian hotel septic-tank passed by in all its stinking splendour, there were good-natured jeers and nose-holdings from the men on shore; they were answered by the rude gestures of their smelly but equally good-natured friends on board. If Venice sits sparkling and indolent upon the morning waters when the tourists wake up, it is only because someone has already done the dirty work, the hauling and heaving, the mucking out and resupplying, that keeps the city going.

Of all the *topo* outfits pressed for time, Barich was one of the most pressed. It didn't carry fish or wine or dirty laundry. It was a courier service, a sort of floating UPS guaranteeing the fastest waterborne delivery possible. Its employees, who regarded themselves as the upper class of delivery men, had to hustle hard for the privilege – each boat made up to 300 separate deliveries a day. In the lead-up to Christmas things were even busier.

As I shook hands with Rene Barich his crews weren't simply passing their documents and parcels from hand to hand – that wasn't fast enough. Standing in the back of a truck reversed onto the quay, the deliveries dispatcher was lobbing smaller packages through the air with all the verve of an American football quarterback firing off snap-passes. Each *topo* was assigned a different *sestiere*, or district, of Venice; shouting out the name of the *sestiere*, he would simultaneously send the object winging off through space to the boat concerned. The crewman standing on its slippery decks had to be fast to catch his package, stow it out of the rain, and be ready and waiting for the dispatcher's next projectile, possibly intended for him. In the mornings I spent at Tronchetto I saw a few spectacular saves, but never a single package dropped in the water or even fumbled.

Moustachioed, greying, Rene Barich was twenty-five years older than his athletic young employees. He ran the office ashore, and he worked hard – he showed up on the quayside early each morning like everyone else. He got along well with his crews because he was like them: he'd risen through the ranks and made good, but he was a local boy. There was no other way to do it.

'Rene Barich is pure Venetian,' Daniel said to me, as we pulled away in the *Alvise*, the 24-foot wooden *topo* I'd been assigned to. 'It doesn't matter how rich you are or where you came from, there are three professions in this city you can't buy your way into. If you want to be a gondolier, a water-taxi driver or a *topo* man you have to be Venetian, born and bred.'

I repeat this exchange as if Daniel had been talking to me in English as the two of us sat in armchairs calmly facing each other in a quiet room. In fact Daniel, ringed of ear and pierced of nose, larded his Italian with Venetian slang and banged it out at high speed. He shouted it to me, as he shouted bits and pieces of information to me all through the morning, through wind and driving rain over the hammering of a marine-diesel engine. Luckily, Daniel had a spare rain-jacket for me. It not only kept me dry but it allowed me to hear him – after a few minutes in the howling gale my heavy-duty garbage bag was reduced to ragged bits of flapping and fluttering plastic.

It didn't matter if I didn't understand everything Daniel said or not. From the moment we turned a watery corner into the Grand Canal there were other voices out there, too, and I heard them perfectly well – the storm beating at the water-stained palazzi that stretched away on either side of us, the hoarse greetings snatched by the wind from topo crews heading past us in the opposite direction, the angry hum of a million raindrops hitting the water all around us. Standing beside Daniel in the *Alvise*'s open stern-well, I didn't mind that my fingers were numb with cold or that icy water was trickling down my chest inside my shirt. All these sounds were telling me there was only one way to see Venice: from the rear of a *topo* heading down the Grand Canal in a rainstorm at 6.30 on a windy morning. There was nowhere else I wanted to be.

The euphoria wore off as the morning progressed, but still I preferred *topo*s to tour-groups. I don't know how many items we delivered. I couldn't possibly remember the route we followed along dozens of canals. And I certainly couldn't recall the streets we followed deep into the heart of the *sestiere* of Dorsoduro. Every time we tied up we would remove the wooden planks covering the hold of the *Alvise*, pull a stainless steel wheeled dolly off the bow, and load it with dozens of packets and parcels. Then we would plunge off into what for me was unknown, unexplored Venice.

'*Attenzione*! *Attenzione*!' Daniel would cry as we made our way through narrow alleys, our passage complicated by the deadly umbrellas that congested them. There is no place like a crowded Venetian thoroughfare in a rainstorm for losing an eye. '*Avanti*! *Avanti*!' I would shout as I helped the dolly up and over the steps of a humpbacked bridge. But neither of these obstacles was as challenging as hunting down the houses to which our packages were destined.

For the Venetian house-numbering system is not like any other in the world. Instead of assigning each street with a new set of numbers, the Venetians count buildings consecutively through an entire *sestiere*. Thus in the *sestiere* of San Marco the Doge's Palace is No. 1 San Marco, while the last house numbers in the 5,000s. In between is an endless maze of criss-crossing alleys, passages, lanes and courtyards, at whose intersections the steadily increasing numbers can meander off in any direction. Daniel had been making courier deliveries for six years, and often he still found it baffling. And bafflement is bad when you're in a hurry – every minute lost is a minute to be made up by the end of the day.

By noon I'd walked miles, hopped ashore with the *Alvise*'s bow line a dozen times, and searched for countless house numbers. We had delivered textbooks to universities, dentures to dentists, legal briefs to law courts, tubes of blueprints to architectural firms. We'd been inside a noisy children's crèche, a steamy restaurant kitchen, a ceramic tile-furnisher's showroom, a dance studio, a carnival sequin supplier's, an ancient bookbinding shop and a funeral home. We had penetrated draughty and half-ruined private palazzi, snug luxury hotels, a casino, an art auctioneer's and a prison. I saw more of Venetian life in one morning than I had seen in three weeks. No one gets around the city and its hidden places more handily than a *topo* driver.

Even Venetian delivery men eventually find time for lunch. In Arca, the little restaurant where the Barich crews met most days at a long table at the back of the room, pizza was taken as seriously as *topo* work. As they downed massive, molten pizzas laden with raw prosciutto they talked. What do Venetian *topo* workers talk about? Like workmen on breaks everywhere, about women. Like most Venetians, about the dismal performance of the city's football team, Venezia Calcio. And, perhaps unlike anyone else at all, about inboard-motor piston-ring specifications, marine crankshaft lubrication, and the idiocy of the water-cops who enforce Venetian canal speed limits. It's hard not to talk shop at lunch.

Afterwards I jumped ship and joined Paolo to make deliveries further across the lagoon. If Daniel was all talk of football and boat engines and his slinky girlfriend Chiara, Paolo was a little older and more contemplative. We braved heavy rain in the *sestiere* of Castello, bounced through rough chop on the way out to Murano, fought the wind on the way back around Venice to Giudecca. It was fraught and soggy, and only after we had dropped off a consignment on a Lido quay late that afternoon did things calm down. The wind died and the rain let up. Abruptly, as we were cruising past Saint Elena on the approaches to Saint Mark's Basin, a single bolt of sunshine shot down through the black clouds above to light upon the surface of the lagoon.

It was dramatic, a dark, stormy seascape pointed with gold and silver. Paolo was as tired and wet as I was but the sight entranced him. He slowed the engine just to watch it for a moment.

'Don't you ever get tired of Venice?' I asked in my

broken Italian. 'To me it seems not real, an extraordinary place in a dream.'

His freckled face, framed in ruddy hair tied back in a rain-soaked bandana, broke into a smile. 'I see this every day,' he said. 'It is normal reality. And still I'm like you. I think it is an extraordinary place, like a dream.'

I told him about other Venices I had seen – Little Venice in London; Venice Beach in California; Amsterdam, Venice of the North. He accepted their attractions, acknowledged they might well have a history and life of their own. 'But none of them,' he said, 'none of them could have a life like Venice. There is nowhere else I could live.'

By now we were in the Basin, and from the mouth of the Grand Canal there emerged three gondolas, their gondoliers taking advantage of the first dry weather of the day to take a party of Japanese tourists over the water. In the lead gondola, facing backwards to a beaming audience, were an accordion player and a tenor singing 'O Solo Mio'. It made the music that issued from the battery-operated gondolas sold on the trinket stalls on the Rialto sound almost good.

Paolo screwed up his face and smiled again. 'You may not believe me, but nothing, nothing at all could make me want to live anywhere else.'

Sixteen

The days slipped by, the rain continued to fall, and life on the *topo*s came to seem like something I'd always been part of. It was one of the rainiest springs Venice could remember. Every day I was wet and cold and every evening I was overheated in the crowded, smoky *osterias* where we ate. After a while delivery by boat became too much of the same thing to be able to distinguish one day on the water from another. I did it instead by remembering meals and the places they were eaten – a terrific dish of squid in its own ink at the Vedova, an especially savoury sausage on polenta at the Bomba. Then, around mid-May came something more memorable still: *aqua alta* – high water.

Nothing special marked the beginning of the

day. At Tronchetto Marcello had clowned around with a rendition of 'Singin' in the Rain', complete with twirlings of an umbrella and swinging around a lamppost. I liked working with Marcello not only because he spoke good English – it relieved me of using bad Italian and an Esperanto nowhere as good as Jany's – but also because he'd seen what life could be off the canals: he'd worked as an orderly in a psychiatric hospital and counselled in a clinic for teenage drug-addicts. Incurably cheerful, Marcello counted himself a lucky man.

He was also the hardest worker at Barich. He had a phenomenal memory, and was faster with difficult addresses than anyone else.

'I am the *putana* of the Barich employees,' he told me happily one morning when he was switched from working the Castello *sestiere* to San Polo. 'Paolo, Daniel and the others only know one *sestiere* and are faithful to them – they don't go anywhere else. I know them all. So when someone goes sick I'm the one called to replace him. I am the *putana* who whores around all Venice.'

Marcello's memory for numbers was so developed that he knew most public places better by their postal addresses than their names. Walking together, I would sometimes test him.

'Dorsoduro 3757,' I would say.

'The Arca restaurant,' he would fire back without a second's hesitation.

'San Polo 3002?'

'The State Archives.'

'San Marco 1243?'

'The Luna Baglioni Hotel.'

But it wasn't numbers above doorways that Marcello was scanning as we tied up outside the Santa Lucia railway station on this mid-May morning. It was the water in the canal below us.

'What is it?' I asked, watching him minutely inspecting water swirling against the wall of the quay where we had docked.

'Nothing,' he said, still watching as the rain spat down on us. 'The tide seems to be running faster than usual, that's all.'

It wasn't five minutes later, as Marcello was asking

a news-kiosk owner in the station for a signature of receipt, that a siren began a low, loud moaning. Like every one else Marcello stopped talking and listened in silence. Then he shook his head, looking troubled. 'It's a flood warning – the *aqua alta* siren. But there shouldn't be any high tides at this time of year. They come in winter.'

'Well, that's no problem for us,' I said cheerfully. 'We're in a boat. We float.'

Marcello looked at me for a long moment, the greenest deliveryman he'd ever worked with.

'We float too much,' he finally said. 'Just try running a *topo* under a canal bridge in *aqua alta*. You'll leave your head and the superstructure of your boat in the water behind you.'

Back on the Grand Canal we stopped in at the Municipio in the Palazzo Loredan. In the lobby on the ground floor there was a sophisticated piece of machinery that gave the current height of the water and a forecast of exactly how high above the average high-tide mark the *aqua alta* would rise. The bright red figure on the current-height display was increasing by the minute. Pushed to the end of the Adriatic by the strong sirocco that had been blowing for days, augmented by ceaseless rains, the waters of the noon high tide were forecast to rise to 115 centimetres above average. It would be enough to flood the lowest-lying parts of the city.

An hour later seawater was overflowing the tops of the canal-banks and spilling out into the city behind. With water climbing the streets we no longer stepped from our *topo* onto dry land, but into a cloudy green soup that rose to our knees. Marcello lent me an old spare pair of the hip-waders that all *topo* crews carry, but they didn't do much good – the rubber had perished and within minutes there were litres of water slopping around inside.

Metal walkways raised two feet off the ground were installed along major pedestrian routes in the city. Shopkeepers and ground-floor residents busied themselves in a flurry of last-minute barrage-building. They slid steel gates into rubber-rimmed flanges running around the lower edges of their door frames, screwed them tight, and gave the joins a quick brush of silicone stopper. Then they waited to see if their entrances would remain watertight.

We didn't help much. Stepping over dammed-up doorways, we sloshed in leaving dark, wet trails wherever we went – the water that had collected in my waders drained out onto every polished floor and carpet I walked on. It seeped onto the tiling in the law courts, dripped onto the meticulously waxed floor-surface of the ladies' lingerie department in the Coin department store, and dribbled into puddles in the geriatric ward in the ancient *Ospedale Civile*.

But nobody took much notice of the mess. They were far more interested in getting the latest news on the flood outside – soon they'd be on their way home to lunch.

'How's the water out there?' they would ask.

'Wet, very wet,' Marcello would reply, as if Venetian water was possessed of properties that more ordinary water was lacking.

The tide rose, hit the promised 115 centimetre mark, caused minor havoc among those Venetians and tourists unprepared for a late spring flood, and then subsided. That evening, sitting in the Portega over *baccalà mantecato* and white wine, we watched the entire bar came to a halt as once again the *aqua alta* siren began its low moan. This time the water would rise to 125 centimetres. When we ordered more wine and some little crabs cooked with lemon and parsley we were served, but also warned to get back to Cannaregio well before high tide at midnight.

But even at ten o'clock we failed to return dryfooted. The Fondamenta Nuove was wholly impassable and the back streets further inland inundated, too. You can always tell locals from tourists in a flood. The Venetians, equipped with knee-high rubber boots when they go out, see *aqua alta* as an unfortunate inconvenience. The foreigners, especially those returning from winey restaurant dinners to their hotels, find it romantic, or hilarious, or both. As we made our way home we crossed paths with men grinning like small boys as they ploughed along through calf-high water, their trouser legs rolled up and shoes and socks held aloft. The women they were carrying on their backs found the whole thing even funnier.

Roberto Puppo didn't find it so amusing. He had to get up before dawn to begin baking but now, as dark water lapped ever higher about his doorsill, he was busy installing and waterproofing his doorway. Two or three doors down a neighbour's daughters had failed to arrive home before their apartment was sealed up. Now they came begging a ladder from Puppo's and, leaning it against an outside wall, climbed to a first-floor window and slithered in, head-first and giggling. From our own first-floor window an hour or two later I looked out to see the street completely flooded. Later, asleep, I had a dream that all I had to do to make a delivery anywhere in the city was lean over the side of the *Alvise* and slide my packet through a window. Jany said it was a dream with deep Freudian implications. I said it was just a *topo* crewman's fantasy – those delivery dollies are hard work.

The next morning there was yet a third *aqua alta* warning for the following high tide. I went down to Tronchetto as usual but asked for the day off. I had three good reasons. For the first time in a week it had stopped raining, and that alone was worth celebrating. Second, I wanted to see the Piazza under water. And third, Jany would soon be flying back to Aix-en-Provence and I setting off in the other direction for Istanbul. I wanted us to see the city together one last time.

We wandered down towards Saint Mark's, where the crowds were thicker than ever. Flooded streets had reduced access to the square to just two or three points, and everyone was jammed on to the raised metal walkways that bordered the Piazza. The square itself was an open lake, as calm and flat as a millpond, its surface reflecting the ragged grey sky and the arcades that surrounded it.

Nothing, though, was going to stop the main business at hand, the purveying of art and culture to the world at large. In front of the Basilica a walkway stretched out of sight around the corner, its human load slowly, patiently moving forward to Venice's very heart. Another walkway carried more visitors, anxious to see the flooded square from above, to the door of the Campanile. Where the two paths crossed there was, inevitably, a traffic jam. Policewomen in rubber boots and dark blue raincoats splashed up and down beside the walkways blowing whistles, gesturing furiously and, as I myself had grown fond of doing, shouting '*Avanti! Avanti!*'

Jany took my hand. 'It's romantic, isn't it?' she asked.

I was going to splutter something sharp and cynical. But I held off because this might be the last time we looked at Venice together, and such moments are supposed to be tender. So instead I simply looked down to the reflecting water in front of me and in it considered the extravagant pavilions of the Basilica, the gorgeous tracery on the Doge's Palace, the winged lion on his granite column in front of Saint Mark's Basin.

And slowly it dawned upon me that Jany was right. The city might no longer be a seat of power, a display of unimaginable wealth, or a jumping-off spot for the East. The great era of its truly cosmopolitan existence was long over, the age of its maritime dominance past. Not even the Mediterranean itself was the great sea it used to be. Despite the changes the world has brought to it, though, Venice remains what it has been from the beginning.

'Yes,' I answered, 'It's romantic.'

A day later Jany was on a plane home to Aix-en-Provence and I was back travelling on *terra firma*. For me, if not for the trading ships of the Serene Republic, Venice remained a jumping-off spot for the East. Perhaps traces of that old cosmopolitan existence lay that way still. I was headed to Istanbul.

Reference Notes

Part of the vast literature of the history of the eastern Mediterranean, I have quoted from the following handful of books, indispensable to any sensible view of three global cities.

1) *Venice* (Faber and Faber: 1993) is Jan Morris's paean to the island-city. It is lush, literate and invaluable, a treasure-trove of both Venetian arcana and style as ornately decorative as the city itself. In addition to quoting her lyric description of Venetian lions I have made use of her knowledge of the Venice state archives, the visit to Venice of the French king Henry III, Venetian streets and canals, and the legend of Saint Mark. A second volume by Morris, *The Venetian Empire – A Sea Voyage* (Penguin: 1990) left me

indebted to Morris for her insight into the Venetian commercial ethos, Enrico Dandolo's sack of Constantinople, and the strategy behind the establishment of Venice's maritime empire.

2) Nicetas Choniates' account of the Frankish profanation of Hagia Sophia in 1204 is cited by John Julius Norwich in *A History of Venice* (Penguin: 2003). For decades the standard English work of Venetian history, its 650 pages are replete with ambitious Venetian personalities, labyrinthine domestic politics and complex international relations. Among other stories I am grateful to Norwich for his accounts of the theft of the body of Saint Mark from Alexandria, the origins of the Sposalizio del Mar, the presence of Miguel Cervantes at the Battle of Lepanto, the functioning of the Venice Arsenal, the death of Pope Pius II in the port of Ancona, and, seen from a greater height, the historic shift in world power from the Mediterranean to the Atlantic.

VENICE.

VENEZIA.
VENEDIG.

Published under the Superintendence of the Society for the
Diffusion of Useful Knowledge.

SCALES

NOTE.